The Family Caregiver's Guide is .... all caregivers, whether family or professional. Harriet Hodgson backs up each chapter topic with an impressive list of resources. Her personal stories add credibility to this research. The Smart Steps at the end of the chapters are excellent. Although Harriet writes about the challenges of caregiving, she also writes about its positive impact on her life. A Registered Nurse and certified counselor, I worked in home health for ten years and was a caregiver for my mother and husband. *The Family Caregiver's Guide* is the best caregiving book I have ever read. I hope it is required reading for all professionals and available to families everywhere.

Mary Amundsen, BSN,
MS Counseling, Caregivers' Support Group Leade

Harriet's latest work is grounded in an honest approach to the full spectrum of what it takes to care. Her focus on the daily realities caregivers have to contend with is a refreshing perspective and one that caregivers at any stage could benefit from reading.

Adrienne Gruberg, President/Founder, The Caregiver Space,
www.thecaregiverspace.org

Harriet Hodgson's latest book, *The Family Caregiver's Guide*, immediately put me at ease. The chapters are well organized. Checklists and questions, sprinkled throughout the book, give the reader opportunities to reflect about caregiving. Smart Tips at the end of each chapter act as a review of information. This is a must-read for new and experienced caregivers alike. Harriet has much to share with the caregivers of the world.

Mary Jane Cronin, MA, LMHC,
Cronin Counseling and Coaching, Largo, Florida,
www.cronincounseling.com

Harriet Hodgson has written many books about heart-wrenching events and does it again with *The Family Caregiver's Guide*. The book is based on her eighteen years of caregiving experience. Harriet was her mother's caregiver, twin grandchildren's caregiver/guardian, and is her disabled husband's caregiver today. Readers will benefit from the guide's clear organization, extensive research, friendly writing, and 101 Smart Steps. Caregivers need all the help they can get. I would recommend *The Family Caregiver's Guide* to any caregiver. It's a winner!

Gloria Horsley, MFC, CNS, PhD,
Cofounder and President of the Open to Hope Foundation,
Co-Host of Open to Hope Radio and Television

The Family Caregiver's Guide is an informative resource for caring for an infirmed loved one. As a nursing professional and caregiver for my daughter, who sustained severe anoxic brain injury more than twelve years ago, I would have welcomed this easy-to-read guide. Even though I'm a RN, with a doctorate in public health systems management, when my daughter was injured I felt overwhelmed. *The Family Caregiver's Guide* provides simple, easy-to-follow steps for caring for a loved one. The appendix contains checklists for creating a safe home environment and definitions of common medical terms. I love the personal touch Harriet Hodgson provides throughout the book, assuring caregivers that we are not alone to fend for ourselves in this chaotic healthcare maze. Each caregiver's journey is personal, and the ability to go to any chapter when needed is a precious gem of this guide. I highly recommend *The Family Caregiver's Guide* to professional and lay caregivers alike, because no caregiver should embark on this journey alone.

Deborah Anzalone, Dr. PH, RN, CHES,
Lighthouse Point, Florida

Just when I think I've got this "caregiving" thing in control, Harriet Hodgson has come up with answers to issues and questions I haven't confronted yet. *The Family Caregiver's Guide* is filled with practical information that can be used to chart schedules, identify problems, and solve problems, all the while taking care of myself. Hodgson is as creative as to have you mentally reverse roles with the person you are caring for, and as practical as to encourage ten minutes of meditation a day for the caregiver. This book is presented differently than any other I've read on caregiving, and may be the only help book I'll need from now on.

Peggy Trumbo,
dementia caregiver on the caregiver journey

The Family Caregiver's Guide

How to Care for a Loved One at Home

Harriet Hodgson, MA

Medical Consultant
C. John Hodgson, MD

Published in the United States by WriteLife Publishing
(An imprint of Boutique of Quality Books Publishing Company)
www.writelife.com

Printed in the United States of America.
Library of Congress Control Number: 2015933443

978-1-60808-126-4 (p)
978-1-60808-127-1 (e)

Book design by Robin Krauss, www.bookformatters.com.
Cover design by Dave Grauel, www.davidgrauel.com.
Cover photo, "Love from Ephesus" from www.istockphoto.com, family photos by Haley Earley.

Thank You

When I started this book I did not know it would turn into a family project. Thank you to my husband, John, for his inspiration, encouragement, and medical expertise. Thank you to my granddaughter, Haley Earley, for taking the photos. Thank you to my grandson, John Welby, for his technical support. And thank you to my daughter, Amy Hodgson, for indexing the book. I am blessed to have such a loving and supportive family.

Also by Harriet Hodgson

*Alzheimer's - Finding the Words: A Communication
Guide for Those Who Care*
available from John Wiley & Sons and Amazon

The Alzheimer's Caregiver: Dealing with the Realities of Dementia
available from Amazon

Smiling through Your Tears: Anticipating Grief
with coauthor Lois Krahn, MD
available from Amazon

Writing to Recover: The Journey from Loss and Grief to a New Life
available from Centering Corporation and Amazon

Writing to Recover Journal
available from Centering Corporation

The Spiritual Woman: Quotes to Refresh and Sustain Your Soul
available from Centering Corporation

*101 Affirmations to Ease Your Grief Journey:
Words of Comfort, Words of Hope*
available from Amazon

Seed Time: Growing from Life's Disappointments, Losses, and Sorrows
available from Amazon

Walking Woman: Step-by-Step to a Healthier Heart
available from Amazon

Happy Again! Your New and Meaningful Life After Loss
available from WriteLife Publishing

Affirmations for Family Caregivers: Words of Comfort, Energy, and Hope
available from WriteLife Publishing

Dedication

This guide is dedicated to all family caregivers,
the unsung heroines and heroes of life.
Thank you for your loving care.

Contents

About This Guide

The goal of this guide is to make caregiving easier for you. When caregiving is easier, you feel more confident and more in control.

Caregiving may be new to you. It may be a second job for you. To become a caregiver, you may have switched to part-time work or quit working. Life is different now. It doesn't take long for you to realize that caregiving duties add up quickly. Busy days become busier. Small worries turn into big worries. The funny, kind person you remember from childhood, now in your care, may become grumpy and difficult.

Over time, fatigue sets in and takes a toll. Like many family caregivers, you don't get enough sleep. You won't be the first caregiver to ask, "Will I survive all this?" Caregiving is a journey, and this book is your guide. The information presented here is reliable, and the stories are real. This book is written and designed for easy reading. Four methods used in this book help to speed you on your way.

1. Chapter titles get straight to the point of addressing the common challenges that caregivers face.

2. Bold headings serve to keep you on course, so that you always know where you are in the contents and where you are headed.

3. Bulleted sections make it easy for you to skim the text and quickly find the information you are seeking.

4. The Appendix is your planning helper. It contains a "Home Safety Checklist," "Medicine Cabinet Supplies" list, and "Terms to Know" list. In addition, at the book's end, the bibliography contains a comprehensive list of sources you can consult for further help, and the index allows you to find what you need in the book.

You don't have to read this guide in one sitting and may begin with any chapter. If you are pressed for time, you may want to head straight for the Smart Steps at the end of the chapters. These are easy-to-find, shaded pages. Taking one Smart Step can save you hours; taking all 101 Smart Steps in this guide may save you days.

Where to Find Smart Steps in this Book

Chapter	Smart Step page
1	Defining your mission: p. 13
2	Fostering hope: p. 28
3	Getting help: p. 40
4	Communicating well: p. 53
5	Attending to your physical and spiritual self: p. 66
6	Gaining self-confidence: p. 79
7	Modifying your home: p. 93
8	Getting equipped: p. 104
9	Looking at your experience: p. 116

I have refrained from writing yet another caregiving memoir. Instead, I have written a guide based upon my life experience and research findings. An old adage says writers write about what they know. This saying is true for me. I have been a health and wellness writer for more than thirty-six years. Most important, I have extensive caregiving experience: I was my mother's caregiver for nine years, I took care of my twin grandchildren for seven years, and I am my husband's caregiver now. He served as the medical consultant for this guide, and his input influenced the content.

Now, let me tell you a little more about my experience.

When my mother was in her eighties, she had a series of mini-strokes that caused dementia similar to Alzheimer's. Her primary care physician didn't order expensive mental tests for her because, as he noted, "We already know the results." Though she lived in a senior community with many support services, I was in charge of her health care, finances, and activities. Whether it was picking up medications, taking her to lunch once a week, making medical and dental appointments, or having her for Sunday dinner, I did something for my mother almost every day. I didn't realize how exhausted I was until she died, and it took a year for me to regain my strength.

John, my husband, practiced medicine for fifty-six years. He has a master's degree in public health, and because of his current medical problems, he knows what it is like to be in need of care. On October 27, 2013, his aorta dissected, and he had three emergency operations. When he was wheeled into surgery the third time, he knew the odds he was facing. There was a twenty percent chance that he might die and a ten percent chance that he might suffer a spinal stroke, which would result in paralysis of his legs. As it turned out, he was in the ten percent group and will spend the rest of his days in a wheelchair. After being hospitalized for eight months, he was discharged to my care.

So, you see, caregiving isn't a new experience for us. John and I are a caregiving team, two people who understand the craziness of your days, the challenges you face, and many of the feelings you feel.

All family caregivers have common tasks, yet each person's journey is unique. Your caregiving journey may be one of the most meaningful experiences of your life. However, it can be so long and tiring that you begin to fear you won't last. Before you know it, days have become weeks, and weeks have become months. The passing of time is just one reason to care for yourself, and this guide helps you do it. Well-meaning family members and friends will give you advice on how to be a caregiver—some of it good, some of it not so good. When all is said and done, you're the expert, the one in the caregiving trenches, and finding your own way. Many days you will feel isolated and alone. You don't have to feel this way. A myriad of services are available to you and they are detailed in successive chapters.

For you, being a family caregiver may only be a possibility, just beginning, or you may already have an established caregiving routine. At six in the morning you get up, help your loved one dress, serve nutritious meals and snacks, plan activities, provide transportation, and help your loved one get ready for bed at night. Your routine may be so established you run on autopilot. During your caregiving journey, I hope you'll laugh, enjoy some hobbies, pursue new interests, and savor the miracle of life. This guide doesn't have to end when you reach the last page. Caregiving links us together, and I welcome your questions and comments. Send them to harriethodgson@charter.net and I will reply as soon as possible. I look forward to hearing from you. Thank you for your loving care.

Introduction

"I never thought I'd be doing this."

You may have heard someone say these words or have said them yourself. Maybe you thought you could avoid assuming the role of caregiver. Caregiving wasn't part of your life plan, and someone else would do it. Your father would care for your mother. Or your mother would care for your father. Aunt Susie would care for her sister. Then circumstances changed, and now you're "it," tagged by one of life's surprises. Caregiving is a huge job, and more families and friends are doing it.

Today newspapers and magazines are running many stories about caregiving. Television viewers are bombarded with ads for home health-care products and services. Some ads run several times an hour, day after day, week after week, and you're tired of seeing them. Perhaps you have received mail about home health-care agencies in your community. Why is all this happening?

Due, in part, to medical and technological advances, the number of older adults in our nation increased markedly in the last ten years. Many communities don't have enough nursing homes for those people who need them. Nursing homes have waiting lists, and moving up on a list can take months or years. As soon as a unit becomes available, it is occupied within days. Older adults appreciate the nursing home's medical services, activity programs, and the gentle care they receive. "This is a good place," a nursing home resident told me. "They take good care of me, and I'm happy here."

Assisted living may be viewed as a type of home care. This approach encourages independent living under a protective umbrella of services. Financial options vary from state to state. Residents may pay additional fees for meals, transportation, parking, activity programs, overnight trips, storage lockers, and health-care services. In some cases, residents are assessed for building improvements. Many assisted living communities offer a "continuum of care" that includes nursing care, hospice care, and end-of-life care. As with nursing home care, the demand for assisted living services exceeds supply, so builders are racing to construct new facilities.

In my hometown of Rochester, Minnesota, senior living communities are popping up like mushrooms. Rochester is the home base of the Mayo Clinic, and its presence may be a reason for the construction surge here. Existing senior-living communities are renovating and expanding. While these communities are needed, some seniors don't welcome them. One local project is being built several miles from my home. Every time I drive past it, I am amazed at how the building keeps getting larger. It is in a prime location that overlooks a river and has a fancy design, but my friends and I have no interest in living there. As one said, "I refuse to live in a warehouse."

For many older adults, and for younger ones, too, home health care is the best solution to a family problem. Pricey as home care is, caring for a loved one at home usually costs less than a nursing home. An article entitled "Comparing Costs for In-Home Care, Nursing Care, Assisted Living, and Adult Day Care," on the *Our Parents* website, says that nursing home care can cost more than $70,000 a year for a semi-private room. The cost of a private room can be more than $79,000 a year—and costs continue to rise.

Familiarity with surroundings may be the main reason for the surge in home health care. Patients who are seriously ill, chronically ill, and terminally ill feel more comfortable in their own homes for good reasons. They know the floor plan, have a favorite chair, and enjoy home-cooked meals. They can interact with family members and are comfortable with the neighborhood. Home health care can be as relaxed as a pair of old slippers. Folks feel at home because they are home.

Family caregiving is new to many people, yet it goes back centuries. Quite a few cultures revere older adults for their experience and wisdom. Grandparents are part of the fabric of family life, and grandmothers are often in charge of raising infant children. Earlier in our history, American families followed this pattern. Grandma, grandpa, a maiden aunt, distant uncle, or orphaned children lived with the family, ate meals with family members, helped with housekeeping, babysat kids, tended the garden, and sat on the porch in the evenings. All of this arrangement was "normal."

Family caregiving has become the new normal, a national trend that prevails from coast to coast. National statistics bear out the growth of caregiving. Some of the numbers are stunning. Here are a few examples from "Caregiving Statistics," an article on the Caregiver Action Network website (www.caregiveraction.org/statistics):

- According to a November 2009 National Alliance for Caregiving report prepared in collaboration with the American Association for Retired Persons (AARP), some sixty-five million people in the United States—twenty-nine percent of the entire population—provide care for a chronically ill or disabled or aged family member or friend during each year.
- About fifty-nine to seventy-five percent of all caregivers are female, notes a 2003 Health and Human Services report to Congress.
- A National Public Radio (NPR) report, "Discovering the True Cost of At-Home Caregiving," says the average age at death in the United States has increased from sixty-eight years to seventy-nine years. "As a result, the personal cost of caring for the elderly at home is rising," the report notes.

Caregiving may have come at a bad time for you. Perhaps you have health problems of your own. Other issues, such as a new mortgage, being a victim of "downsizing," or the re-zoning of your neighborhood, can affect the care you provide. In the book, *Passages in Caregiving*, author Gail Sheehy (2010) describes caregiving as a collision between conflicting stages of life. This may be true for you. You may not have expected this collision and have been caught off-guard by it. While you're caring for your loved one, you must figure out how to care for yourself. Talk about a challenge!

Trial and error are your teachers, and the lessons can be painful. You may have assumed a parental role for your ailing father—an uncomfortable role, to be sure. Often spousal caregivers may find themselves switching roles. A wife who relied on her husband to pay bills and do the taxes may be forced to take over these tasks or hire professional help. A husband who never fried an egg may wind up preparing meals for his wife. Family caregiving is a journey filled with detours, wrong turns, and surprises.

If your loved one has a chronic illness, you face the reality of her or his physical degeneration. This process can be rapid or prolonged. You might think you know how long you will be a caregiver, but there's no sure way of knowing. The journey can last for years. During the nine years I was my mother's caregiver, I felt as if she were dying cell by cell before my eyes. At the time, I didn't know about anticipatory grief, didn't know its symptoms, and didn't understand its power. The day my mother failed to recognize me was one of the worst of my life.

I had gone to visit her in nursing care, and, when I approached her bed, her eyes widened in fear. Mom made loud grunting sounds (she could barely speak by then) and pushed me away. Apparently she thought I was a stranger who intended to harm her. During subsequent visits, she continued to make these sounds and push me away. Then Mom started to refuse food. When she refused water, I knew the end was near. The head nurse said my mother's body was "shutting down," so I made an agonizing decision, one based on love for my mother (my champion, my biggest fan, and my role model). I wanted my mother to die peacefully, not fearfully, so I stopped visiting her, stayed home, and sobbed. A day and a half later, my mother died.

You may have made a painful decision, such as the one I made. Maybe you have made several such decisions, and each one was life changing. Life's agonizing decisions can make you feel down. To balance this situation, pat yourself on the back now and then. Take credit for small things, like making delicious coffee. Take credit for big things, like decorating your loved one's bedroom. Take credit for managing your loved one's finances efficiently. Take credit for loving someone so much it hurts. Each day, remind yourself of this truth: *I am making a difference in someone's life.* Say it aloud, and say it often.

Chapter 1

Caregiving Is an Expanding Role

SMART STEPS: P. 13

Caregiving may be new to you. You may not know what the job entails. Defining your mission is a good place to start. Even if you're an experienced caregiver, you may want to rethink your mission. There may be more to your caregiving job than you first realize. For example, your loved one may have been diagnosed with diabetes. Your spouse's health may decline more quickly than anticipated. Caregiving is doubly difficult if your loved one has dementia. You need to know your mission and stay on task. Is your mission clear in your mind?

Define Your Mission

A caregiver's basic mission is to protect and care for the ill person. Your mission statement may have a qualifier, such as "I will care for my loved one as long as I can."

Why should you bother to think about your mission? Answering this question often leads to thoughts about family issues. A brother or sister may think they should be your loved one's primary caregiver, but your home is better suited for caregiving. You may be in a better financial position to care for a loved one. You may live in the same town as your loved one, whereas siblings live thousands of miles away, and becoming your loved one's caregiver makes more sense. This decision also saves your loved one from an expensive, tiring move.

Your Job Description

So many people are caring for family members, that you would think there would be a standard job description. There isn't. Variations in caregivers, the persons receiving care, and locations make a standard job description impossible. Because no standard job description exists, you may wish to write your own. Writing your own job description has several advantages. For one thing, it helps you clarify your thoughts. Your job description may placate angry family members and can be a source of support when times are tough.

How do you write a job description? Think about the tasks in your day, starting with early morning. Which task takes the most time? Which takes the least? Perhaps you spend a quarter of your day on personal care for your loved one, helping with bathing and dressing. Your job description will be longer if the care receiver has Alzheimer's disease or another form of dementia. Before you start writing, think of the plusses you bring to caregiving, such as past experience. Also consider the following factors about yourself:

- Physical health
- Emotional health
- Strength
- Mobility
- Organizational skills
- Adaptation skills
- Personality
- Level of education
- Budgeting and money management skills
- Special talents

Don't be modest about your talents and skills. They are an important part of you and can be caregiving assets. Still, you have to be realistic. If you have paid caregivers, a topic discussed on page 87–89 of this guide, you may not be doing all the tasks yourself. Review your daily tasks, and make a list of them in order to get organized. Give yourself lots of lead time because developing an inclusive list of tasks may take more time than you anticipated.

I pondered over a job description after I became co-guardian of my twin grandchildren. Our daughter had listed us as their guardians in her will. John and I vowed to do all we could do to help the twins. One thing we decided not to do, however, was attempt to be substitute parents. The twins' parents were loving and caring people. Trying to replace them could hurt the twins and make them resent us. I remember the day I spoke about this problem to my granddaughter. We were in the car, on our way to a friend's house, when I turned to her and said, "I love you and am not trying to replace your mother. Grandpa is not trying to replace your father. We are your grandparents and always will be." Though she did not answer, my granddaughter nodded her head to show she heard me.

Your Task List

Three categories, **Health-Related, Personal,** and **Financial,** are a good foundation for your list. Group your tasks in these categories, so that it is clear to you what you are facing and what you will need help with. Under Health-Related, you may write, "Dispense medications." Under Personal, you may write, "Mail thank-you cards." Under Financial, you may write, "Pay property tax." Jot down every idea that pops into your head. Add other tasks that pertain to your caregiving situation, so that you do not forget what to do. Your task list may contain some unusual notations, such as "Search for Mom's false teeth." While you're making a list of tasks, you may laugh and you may cry.

Toward the end of my mother's life, I acquired some new tasks. One was to look behind the draperies in my mother's nursing care room for food she had squirreled away. And it was usually there: dried chicken wrapped in tissues, bits of beef, half of a dried roll. I couldn't believe the intelligent, organized mother of my childhood was unable to tell spoiled food from fresh. The "squirrel test," as I thought of it in my mind, was an indication of her mental status, and it was going downhill fast.

I also became a hearing aid hunter. Mom threw out two hearing aids worth four thousand dollars, and I didn't want her to lose the new ones I bought. When I visited her in nursing care, I checked the trash can to see if her hearing aids were there. I looked on the bedside table and under the bed. But I was not with my mother all the time, and, much to my dismay, she threw out a second set of hearing aids.

Task lists tend to get longer, and you may think no end is in sight. Like me, you may miss details and points that only become apparent with experience. Tasks can "grow." As an example, I knew I would be doing my husband's laundry every day but didn't know I would do four loads or more. When his shower chair is wheeled out of the bathroom across the bedroom floor, it leaves a trail of drips and little puddles. Mopping up that water trail takes five towels, a load of laundry by themselves. Prescriptions are another example of a growing task. I knew I would have to take John's prescriptions to the drug store and pick them up, but I didn't know refilling some prescriptions required extra lead time.

So check your task list from time to time, and revise it as needed. Also, make sure your loved one's prescriptions are current, what the medications' shelf life is, and who wrote the prescription—a physician, physician's assistant, or physical therapist.

In many ways, caregiving is a balancing act. While you are caring for your loved one, you are fostering her or his independence. Some days, your loved one will be independent; on other days, she or he will be very dependent, and this change may scare you. Watching a loved one struggle to perform simple tasks can be a painful experience. Still, you grit your teeth and follow the doctor's orders to let your loved one do what she or he can. Helping your loved one set goals is another task that should be on your list, one that may lead to long conversations. In time, you and your loved one should be able to set some goals together.

Help with Setting Goals

No matter how old we are, no matter how sick we are, we all need a sense of pride. Doing too much for your loved can dampen her or his pride. Certainly, you don't want your loved one to become discouraged and give up altogether. Your loved one's goals need to be realistic. The goals of someone facing surgery will differ from those of someone who is in rehabilitation. Author Kenneth E. Randall has clarified some of the differences in goals. He is Assistant Professor in the Department of Physical Therapy at the University of Oklahoma Health Sciences Center. Co-author Irene R. McEwen is with the same department.

Randall and McEwen list five components of goal setting in their *Physical Therapy Journal* article, "Writing Patient-Centered Functional Goals." I have added brief explanations to their points.

1. **Who is this person?** This component includes the person's age, medical history, nature and severity of illness, treatments that were tried, and treatments that are planned.
2. **Who will do what?** This component assigns care tasks to professional and family caregivers. Health professionals may work on some tasks together.
3. **Under what conditions will they do it?** This component includes place, personal care plan, type of health insurance, health insurance regulations, and health-care staff.
4. **How well will it be done?** This component focuses on personal goals, such as "I will be able to flex my fingers."
5. **When does it need to be done?** This goal establishes a time frame: two weeks, a month, or several months. Follow-up care may be part of this component.

Whether rehabilitation is in the hospital, nursing home, or at home, rehab is an actual and visionary place. It is a place of challenges, pain, and hope. Physical and occupational therapists base their treatments on one premise: each client will do his or her best to develop skills that foster independence. If your loved one stops making progress (*plateaus* is the term used by health professionals), therapy may cease. To arrange for more therapy, you may have to become more assertive. Encourage your loved one, even if her or his goals seem unrealistic.

John shared his ultimate goal—to use a walker—with the physical therapist assigned to the rehabilitation floor of the nursing home. When

John stated this objective, his therapist was standing behind him, and John could not see his face. But I saw the therapist's surprised expression, saw him start to speak, hesitate, wait a moment, and answer, "That's a worthy goal." His reply was perfect: not demeaning, not unrealistic, but encouraging in a gentle way. John and I can't say enough good things about his physical therapist, the person who refused to give up, kept cheering him on, and taught John how to stand.

Become an Advocate

When you care for a loved one, you are also his or her advocate. Today, many hospitals have patient advocates for family members. Because advocates know the hospital, insurance regulations, and the community, they are able to solve problems that baffle the rest of us. Family members may seek a patient advocate's help because they feel they have been treated unfairly. Family members may seek a patient advocate's help because they are confused. Hospitals and insurance companies are the main employers of patient advocates. As the value of patient advocates becomes more widely known, many businesses are employing them.

Though you may not be a trained advocate, you can assume this role and represent your loved one. Your tasks may be similar to a professional advocate's tasks. Craig Pomykal, a patient advocate with the Texas Health Harris Methodist Hospital in Fort Worth, Texas, describes tasks in his article, "The Emerging Role of the Hospital Patient Advocate." This article was posted on the *Professional Advocate Institute* blog. He compares professional advocates to social workers because they work as generalists and collaborators. You are capable of generalizing and collaborating, too, and your duties may be as far ranging as a professional advocate's.

Becoming John's advocate wasn't on my "To Do" list. As the months passed, however, I eased into the role. I filled out insurance forms, attended care conferences, ordered health-care equipment, picked up equipment, talked with insurance companies, made follow-up phone calls, and set doctors' appointments. John recognized my advocacy and declared, "Advocacy never stops." He is right. Patient advocacy is built into your caregiving mission statement.

Advocacy requires truthfulness. John didn't realize he had Intensive Care Unit (ICU) Psychosis until I pointed it out to him. Years ago, when John was an Air Force flight surgeon, he was ordered to the National Aeronautical and Space Administration (NASA) in Houston, Texas. John hallucinated about this time when he was in the ICU. He thought he was back at NASA, fighting an imaginary foe, and making plans to defend astronauts. Excessive anesthesia caused his confusion and forgetfulness. Though John knew this, he didn't realize how poor his memory had become. Thankfully, as the anesthesia slowly left his body, he became more alert, more realistic, and more aware of my advocacy. He asked, "What happens to people who don't have an advocate?"

Assessment Checklist

To get a better picture of home health care, you may wish to use this checklist, which is based on a "Caregiving Assessment" checklist posted on *WebMD*. I have changed the wording and added extra points to the list. As you can see, this list has two sections, *Care Receiver* and *Caregiver*, and the list gives you a general picture of your situation. You may think of extra points and, if you do, please add them. Put a check by the points that apply to your situation. Doing this will help clarify what caregiving involves for you, and the points you may clarify for others.

Care Receiver

_____ Is confined to bed.

_____ Can be transferred to a wheelchair with a mechanical lift.

_____ Can transfer self to a wheelchair with a transfer board.

_____ Is able to get out on his or her own.

_____ Is unable to feed herself or himself.

_____ Is able to feed herself or himself, using special utensils.

_____ Can come to the table for family meals.

_____ Is unable to bathe herself or himself.

_____ Is able to bathe herself or himself in a shower wheelchair.

_____ Can do the Activities of Daily Living (ADL): bathing, grooming, dressing.

_____ Is unable to control elimination and needs assistance with a bedpan.

_____ Requires catheterization.

_____ Can do self-catheterization.

_____ Uses bathroom independently.

_____ Requires twenty hours or more of personal care per week.

_____ Requires less than ten hours of personal care per week.

_____ Mind and memory are working well.

_____ Is mentally confused.

_____ Is mentally confused sometimes.

_____ Thinks clearly and is able to make competent decisions.

Caregiver

_____ Is in frail or poor health.

_____ Activities are limited.

_____ Is in good general health and is physically active.

_____ Is employed full-time outside the home.

_____ Is employed part-time outside the home.

_____ Has a flexible work schedule.

_____ Isn't employed outside the home.

_____ Works at home.

_____ Is responsible for other family members, including kids.

_____ Is responsible for the person receiving care only.

_____ Has the funds to hire full-time assistance.

_____ Lacks caregiving skills and confidence.

_____ Has adequate caregiving skills and confidence.

_____ Has less than four free hours each week.

_____ Takes one day off per week.

_____ Is able to continue hobbies and activities.

_____ Is willing to sacrifice sleep in order to attend to the receiver's needs.

_____ Sometimes gets less sleep in order to attend to the receiver's needs.

_____ Sleeps well each night and has no sleep problems.

How did you do? Is your caregiving picture clearer, fuzzy, or dark? Many caregivers struggle alone. You may be an only child and thus the only caregiver. Siblings who live thousands of miles away may not be much help. A sibling may come and help for a week or so; while you appreciate the help, it's a drop in the caregiving bucket. Even with paid help, caregiving can be exhausting. In addition to being responsible for your loved one, you are responsible for managing visitors.

Visitors

Visitors can brighten your loved one's day. Unfortunately, some people think they can visit any time, and unexpected visitors can be a monkey wrench in your plans. Diana B. Denholm, PhD, LMHC, describes some of the problems caregivers have with visitors in *The Caregiving Wife's Handbook* (2012). She says visitors can complicate caregiving and throw off our rhythms, something you may have experienced. Surprise visitors can result in missed medication times, poor meals, and sanitary problems. Denholm's solution is to follow a hospital model of no visitors at mealtime, medication times, or treatment times.

Get your loved one involved in planning for visitors, if possible. Does she or he prefer visitors in the morning, afternoon, or evening? Will visitors include infants, toddlers, or teenagers? Will food be served? Does your loved one want to do anything special with the visitors? Maybe your loved one would like to look at photos, plant a container garden, or do a puzzle. To make sure your loved one doesn't get overly tired, keep track of time when visitors are present. Here are some tips that will help visits from family and friends go more smoothly:

1. **Remind.** The day before visitors are to arrive, remind your loved one of these plans. Remind your loved one again on the day of the visit.

2. **Check supplies.** Do you need to extend the dining table or borrow some chairs? Have you checked off everything on your planning list?

3. **Plan the food.** Instead of doing all the cooking, plan a potluck meal or a dessert buffet.

4. **Involve.** Plan a group activity, such as looking at photos. Your loved one may suggest an activity to you.

5. **Change plans.** Don't be afraid to cancel the visit if your loved one doesn't feel well. Family members and friends should understand.

Ask for Help

For some caregivers, getting help is easy: they simply ask for it. However, if you are a stay-in-charge kind of person, asking for help can be hard. You will need help if your loved one is in the final stages of Alzheimer's disease. Ask for help if your loved one requires all day and night care. Ask for help if you're sick. Ask for help if you think you're becoming depressed. Help is available from home health-care agencies, private nurses, the Alzheimer's Association, the American Association of Retired Persons (AARP), other national organizations, senior centers, social service agencies, city governments, colleges, universities, and the Area Council on Aging.

Adult day care may be the solution to your problem. Get information about adult day care, and choose a program that meets your loved one's needs. Talk with families who are using these programs. What do they like most about them? Are there any problems? Does their loved one like the program?

According to the article "Adult Day Care," posted on the *Eldercare Locator* website, the main goal of these programs is to delay or prevent institutionalization. Fostering self-esteem and socialization are also goals. There are two basic types of adult day care: daytime social care and daytime health care. The adult day care center or centers in your town may be located in a senior center, nursing home, church, synagogue, hospital, or school. Be ready to reach for your wallet, because this care can be costly.

According to "Adult Day Care Programs and Costs," an article on the *Home Advisor* website, rates range anywhere from forty to seventy dollars per day, depending on how often your loved one attends. Health-care services and meal programs will increase the daily costs. Yet the costs may be worth the rewards. Adult day care can be a win–win situation for caregivers and the persons receiving care. The department of social services in your community will be able to provide you with more information about the available help in your area.

Affirm Your Role with Words

Many counselors recommend affirmation writing to boost your spirits and reveal hidden thoughts. I recommend it to caregivers. Affirmation writing is similar to writing poetry; it allows you to express yourself freely. This writing can take more time than anticipated. After you have written a few affirmations the process goes more quickly. One-sentence affirmations usually work best because they are easier to remember. You may wish to write an affirmation on a small piece of paper, tuck it in your pocket, and read it later in the day.

- *Taking care of myself makes me a better caregiver.*
- *Laughing with John is an expression of love.*
- *Most of the time, with some exceptions, I speak with a gentle voice and heart.*
- *I benefit from the church caregiving support group and look forward to monthly meetings.*
- *For me, caregiving is a sacred mission.*
- *Being a caregiver teaches me new things about myself.*
- *To better understand caregiving, I imagine myself as the care receiver.*
- *Every moment with John is a gift.*

Affirmation writing can change your caregiving outlook and boost your confidence. You may benefit from writing affirmations so much, you keep on writing them. The more affirmations you write, the better your "self-talk" will be, so keep writing. Start an affirmations notebook or computer file. Print out a special affirmation, and stick it on the refrigerator door. There is no better time to affirm yourself, your role, and your life. Reading your affirmations aloud brings the words to life and strengthens your belief in yourself.

SMART STEPS

- Define your mission and write it down.
- Write a job description.
- Make a list of caregiving tasks. Revise the list when necessary.
- Help your loved one set new goals.
- Become your loved one's advocate.
- Help your loved one plan for visitors.
- Be aware of your limitations.
- Ask for help when you feel swamped.
- Enroll your loved one in adult day care.
- Write caregiving affirmations and keep writing them.

Chapter 2

Focus on the Care Receiver

SMART STEPS: P. 28

Your loved one sees caregiving differently than you do. This view changes if your loved one is hospitalized for a long time or transferred to a nursing home. If health-care agencies get involved in care, your loved one's opinion may change again. You may also worry about opinions from health-care professionals. I felt pressured by one of John's doctors until I realized his requests were based on Medicare regulations.

Family members' views may influence your loved one's view of caregiving. When family members are encouraging, your loved one will probably feel encouraged. When family members are discouraging, your loved one will probably feel discouraged. As much as your loved one wants to be independent, becoming a care receiver is a dependent role. This realization can come as a shock to your loved one and to you.

Unwelcome Role Reversal

How would you feel if you were the person receiving care? Becoming that person would, no doubt, change your conversations, needs, goals, and plans. You would feel as if you had been robbed of your independence. When your loved one became dependent, she or he lost control of normal life. Disappointing as this loss may be, there's a bright spot in this scenario, and it is attitude. A positive attitude is energizing and can change your loved one's feelings. Mike Volpe's story illustrates this point. Volpe tells his story in "The Art of Care Receiving," posted on the *Real Living with Multiple Sclerosis* website.

Volpe has been receiving in-home care for years. A functional quadriplegic, he needs help with the Activities of Daily Living (ADL) and other tasks. By his own admission, Volpe made it difficult for caregivers to do their jobs, and his attitude "reduced their satisfaction of working with me." Then Volpe came to a life-changing decision, and it is one to remember: *Care receiving is an art.* This realization literally changed Volpe's life. It can change your loved one's life too.

Now Volpe accepts help and asks for more when he needs it. He kept his old friends and made new ones. He works hard to keep his health stable, a challenging task for a disabled person. Before, he didn't have a primary care physician, and now he has one. Volpe has a network of caregivers and "a style of care receiving that fits my personality." Most of these inner changes happened unconsciously, Volpe says; and as his thinking changed, he found ways to retain his identity.

While Volpe doesn't reveal these ways, we may imagine them. For example, instead of giving wishy-washy answers to questions, or saying "I don't know," he may have given decisive "yes" or "no" answers. He may have gotten better at expressing his needs. *I need some lotion on my back. I'm thirsty and need a drink of water. I'm hungry and would like to eat lunch early.*

Caring for himself mentally and finding a life purpose are paramount to Volpe. He is now an activist for the disabled. The point of this story is that your loved one may come to a similar conclusion. You may have to talk about this with your loved one. Each day, try to give your loved one choices. *Do you want a hot or cold breakfast? Would you like a snack now? Do you want to play cards, watch television, or read? Are you interested in an online history course? Shall I get your laptop or the new magazine that just came?* Having choices helps your loved one retain a sense of control, however small it may be.

Modesty and Privacy

Privacy disappears when a caregiver helps with baths, showers, and incontinence. In his article, Volpe says there is a difference between *physical privacy* and *mental privacy*. He thinks mental privacy is more important. While nudity can be difficult for the care receiver, you can help by pulling the shower curtain closed and covering parts of your loved one's body with a towel. Your loved one may feel more comfortable if another person—a witness—is present at bath or shower time. This person may be the same sex as your loved one.

Diverting conversations can also help your loved one feel more comfortable during tasks involving being nude. You may talk about the news, family gatherings, or the weather. Using medical terms can also help de-personalize your tasks. Modesty is a difficult issue if your loved one has Alzheimer's disease. As confusion gets worse, some people with Alzheimer's develop a fear of water and think they will drown if they take a bath. You may have to reassure your loved one before bathing time.

Some people with Alzheimer's or other forms of dementia (the same people who were modest all their lives) start walking around nude. My mother did this. Before she moved to Rochester, Minnesota, my mother lived in Florida. Her condominium overlooked a golf course, and golfers walked by constantly. But my mother didn't close the curtains and walked around nude in front of the windows. When I told her this wasn't a good idea because of all the golfers, she replied firmly, "Oh, they can't see me." If she could see the golfers, they could see her, I explained, but my mother didn't believe me.

If nudity is a problem, you may wish to buy several robes and keep them within reach.

Your loved one may not want to bathe at all. Within a few hours, she or he may start to smell. For hygienic reasons, you will have to insist on a bath. When you do this, remember that you're dealing with disease, not the loved one you remember from the past. Each day will be different and, months later, your loved one's actions may make you smile. Consult a gerontologist if nudity and/or the refusal to bathe are caregiving problems.

Modesty is related to privacy. Hiring outside help reduces privacy for everyone. Most states have passed legislation regarding caregiver background checks. The Wisconsin Department of Health Services, for example, has a caregiver law that requires facilities and agencies to complete two types of background checks. The first type is done by employers and contractors, and the second is done by the Division of

Quality Assurance. Other states are recognizing the need for background checks. If your state doesn't have a background-check law, you may wish to purchase a background check from an online source.

Effects of Medications on Memory

Your loved one may have had surgical operations and may have been anesthetized for each one. It can take months for the effects of anesthesia to leave the body. After your loved one leaves the hospital, additional medications may be prescribed, and these medications can affect memory. Some medications shouldn't be taken together, and your primary care physician and pharmacist can give you more information about this danger. As a caregiver, you need to be aware of the side-effects of medications. One medication may cause sleepiness, another may cause dizziness, and another may cause an upset stomach.

Each medication has its own half-life, which is the time it takes for the medication to lose half of its potency in a person's body. Half-life calculations are complex. Although free calculators are available on the Internet, check with a physician or pharmacist about the half-life of each medication. For example, if your loved one doesn't seem "right" to you, it may be due to the anesthesia that is still in her or his body after a surgery. It may be due to drug interactions or the half-life of a medication. Some slow-acting drugs can stay in the body for weeks.

When John was discharged from the nursing home, he still had some short-term memory problems. As the weeks passed, his memory improved and continues to improve. Still, it can take him fifteen minutes to remember something. "I'm slow sometimes," he admits, "but I usually come up with the answer." He does, indeed, have the answers, and his medical knowledge is intact. His wisdom is also intact, and I benefit from it every day. I'm grateful for the return of John's humor and the spark it brings to our marriage. Laughter is a part of every day at our house, and that is a blessing.

Altered Sense of Self

Self-concept is basically defined as how we think of ourselves and behave. But part of our self-concept is also based on our physical abilities. In the past, your loved one may have been a skilled tennis player, but now she or he uses a walker, which is a dramatic life change. Adjusting to a difference such as using a walker can take months. Changes in health can alter your loved one's self-concept. She or he is in a new situation, coping with new challenges, and adjusting as quickly as possible. Old ideas may be reconsidered and, slowly or rapidly, replaced with new ones.

John practiced medicine for forty-eight years. Being a practicing physician was his self-concept. While retirement changed this concept slightly, he still thought of himself as a physician. To confirm this belief, he stayed up-to-date on medical issues, attended conferences, attended retirement functions, and spent time with colleagues. Eight years ago his upper aorta dissected, and surgeons replaced it with a Dacron descending aorta. After the lower part of his aorta dissected in 2013, he let his medical license and narcotics license lapse. These decisions changed John's self-concept.

"I'm not a doctor anymore," he declared.

"You'll always be a doctor," I replied. But I was concerned about him, and this concern is one reason I asked him to serve as the medical consultant for this guide.

"You used to help people in your office," I explained. "Now you can help people with words. Working on the guide would be a good use of your medical knowledge."

"Good idea," he replied enthusiastically. The more he thought about it, the more John liked the idea. Working on the guide could help John keep his self-concept as a physician and help me with my self-concept as a health writer. Best of all, working on the guide was something we could do together. Each of us would bring our experiences and strengths to the project.

You may help your loved one update his or her self-concept. Perhaps your loved one is interested in writing an autobiography, working on a family tree, documenting family history, organizing photos that have been in boxes for years, posting on blogs, or donating a treasured collection to a local museum. Many possibilities are open to your loved one. Families may lose history because a loved one refuses to put memories in writing or record them on a smartphone. What a shame. Please ask your loved one to write about their memories. If your loved one is a two-fingered typist, buy a software program that types spoken words on a computer screen. Helping your loved one update his or her self-concept is a reachable goal.

Feeling Out of Touch

Long-term caregiving can make you feel out of touch. You may rarely see your friends, and, if you do see them, you feel rushed and worry about your loved one. Lack of socialization can lead to depression. How can you stay in touch with others? You may retain membership in some organizations and resign from others. Writing e-mails and posting on Facebook are ways to stay in touch with others. You may even write posts on caregiving blogs. Writing a letter, old-fashioned as it may seem, is an excellent way to stay in touch. The recipient will appreciate the letter and the time you spent writing it.

Finding new means of transportation can make your loved one feel out of touch. This barrier can be difficult to overcome. For two months after John's dismissal from the nursing home, we relied on a wheelchair van service, and the fees were high. We fantasized about getting our own wheelchair van. With help from a home therapist, John learned how to slide on a transfer board from his wheelchair into the front seat of my car. The physical therapist's plan was for John to perfect this skill and for us to buy a lightweight transport chair. After we reached our destination, I would take the transport chair out of the trunk, help him transfer to it and wheel him around.

Until we tested the plan, it seemed workable. The therapist put the chair in the trunk of my car and asked me to remove it. I leaned over, reached for the wheelchair, and felt a sharp pain in my back. "Stop!" she exclaimed. "It's not going to work." Disappointed as he was, John tried to be upbeat, and thanked me for trying. I felt as if I had failed my husband.

We had to find another solution to our transportation problem and, two months later, we bought a used wheelchair van.

Depression Awareness

An older loved one may become depressed. This feeling is not common, according to the Centers for Disease Control and Prevention (CDC). The CDC makes this point in the article, "Depression is Not a Normal Part of Growing Older." More than feeling blue, depression is a bona fide medical illness with many symptoms. These symptoms can be so debilitating that the depressed person thinks about suicide. Family members may not know about their relative's suicidal thoughts until it is too late. That is why it is a good idea to know the symptoms of depression. They include the following signs:

- Pessimistic, hopeless feelings
- Irritability
- Lack of interest in hobbies/activities
- Urge to sleep
- Concentration problems
- Over-eating or under-eating
- Ongoing aches, pains, and digestive problems
- Lack of personality and reactions
- Suicidal comments

While depression in older adults is not common, older adults are at risk for it, according to the CDC. Keep in mind that depressed people may laugh and joke to hide their true feelings.

Do you think your loved one is becoming depressed? Listen carefully to what your loved one says. Watch for the symptoms of depression. Try to engage in activities that foster physical activity. Assure your loved one that she or he is still needed. Ask your loved one how he or she has been feeling lately. The response may reveal new things that you didn't know. Make an appointment with a physician if you think your loved one is depressed.

Depression is the most treatable of all mental illnesses, and help is just an e-mail or phone call away.

New Life Purpose

Quality of life depends, in part, on having a purpose. Becoming a person who receives care doesn't change this fact. Despite the fact that circumstances have changed and your loved one is under your care, she or he still needs a purpose. Life is better when there is a reason to wake up in the morning. Now may be a good time to broach the subject of purpose with your loved one. There are several ways to begin the conversation. I recommend a direct approach.

Talk with your loved one about previous purposes, such as being a good father or mother. This discussion can open a floodgate of memories. Like percolating coffee, memories may bubble up, and you may have a wonderful conversation with your loved one. Could she or he update a prior life mission? Being a person who receives care does not mean your loved one cannot pursue his or her interests. A grandmother may continue to sew clothes. A grandfather may continue to make fly rods. A husband may continue to sing in the church choir.

Sharing expertise may be your loved one's new purpose. Perhaps she or he understands the stock market or investment strategies, and wants to share this knowledge with others. Or, your loved one may be interested in saving animals and can contribute to a local organization devoted to this purpose. At this time of life, your loved one may wish to donate a treasured collection to a history museum. Having a new life purpose can take your loved one in new directions.

Benefits of Humor

Laughter is one of life's miracles. With the exception of laughing hyenas (who do make a laughing sound) I believe humans are the only living creatures that laugh. We all benefit from laughter. In fact, many folks believe laughter helps to heal illness. Medical studies suggest that laughter lowers blood pressure, and sharing a joke makes people feel closer to each other. As you go about your daily tasks, try to see the humorous side of things.

Blogger Angela Lunde thinks humor helps us cultivate resilience. Her post, "Alzheimer's Support Group Gets Lift from Humor, Sharing," expands on this point. While nobody in her Alzheimer's support group solved another's problems or dismissed their emotional pain, they were willing to share their true selves and connect with humor. As Lunde explains, "Humor seemed to ease the hold of the negative emotions and, most importantly, it strengthened the connection amongst the group." Similarly, humor may strengthen your connection with your loved one. There's nothing like laughing with someone you care deeply about.

Sources of Hope

Your husband or wife may be a source of hope. I am moved to tears by my husband's courage. John refuses to give up on life. He cooperates with physicians, nurses, aides, and therapists. For instance, his physical therapist recommended a peddler to us, a device with two pedals that can be operated with hands or feet. We bought one, and John uses it faithfully to maintain upper body strength. Every evening, just before he goes to bed, John peddles with his hands, and his stamina has increased.

"I'll try anything," he declared, "and I'll never give up." His attitude is an ongoing source of hope for me. John is a man of courage, and his courage has never faltered. He is also a source of hope for family members.

University of Minnesota professor Robert L. Veninga, MD, details the importance of hope in his book, *A Gift of Hope: How We Survive Our Tragedies*. At one time or another, you may turn to family for hope. Cohesive families are able to survive tragedy for several reasons. The most striking reason, according to Veninga, is that they are not bitter. Family members live in the present, not the past. They manage conflicts creatively, solve problems together, and give each other room to breathe. Your family members may help you and, at the same time, give you room to breathe.

Medical research is an ongoing source of hope. Researchers have made progress in identifying early signs of Alzheimer's disease, for example, an advancement that gives patients and families more time to plan. Pharmaceutical companies are constantly developing and testing new medications. Thanks to genomics (the discipline in which biotechnology is applied to genetics and molecular biology), patients can receive customized treatments. Inventors have devised new braces for patients who have weak legs.

The chances of John walking again are slim, yet the idea is a source of hope. It gives him something to work toward, and John is willing to do the work. In November, thirteen months after he was dismissed from the nursing home rehabilitation unit, he started rehabilitation at Mayo Clinic. On the first day, the therapist hooked John up to a bike that provides electrical stimulations. His session began with a warm up, and then the therapist increased the speed and stimulation. Fifteen minutes later, the therapist made a stunning announcement. "You're peddling on your own," she said. I couldn't believe what I saw or the words I just heard.

Later sessions yielded the same results. John would warm up, peddle with stimulation, and then peddle on his own. When he used the parallel bars, therapists helped him stand, and they corrected his posture. John used the bars at each session, and the day came when his therapist asked him to "Take a step." John did it! I started to cry, but the therapist grinned. "Merry Christmas!" she exclaimed. Now the goal is to get him to stand and pivot, which would eliminate the need for a transfer board.

Religious and spiritual beliefs may be another source of hope. I give workshops about grief healing, writing, and caregiving. To encourage participation, I asked for suggestions from the group. The topic of stress came up at one session. "I have a God box," a man shared. "Every time I have a worry, I write it on a small piece of paper, and stick it in the box under my bed." Using a God box helped the man manage stress, but the results he described were more interesting. "Months later, when I look at the papers, most of the worries are gone," he said.

You may wish to keep your own box. Prayer and meditation may also be calming. Members of your religious community can provide help when you need it most. For example, because our former home had several flights of stairs, John couldn't return there. I moved us out of the house by myself—a huge, discouraging, and exhausting job. We love books, and the thought of moving hundreds of books to our new place brought me to tears. In desperation, I contacted our church and asked for help. An urgent e-mail went out to parishioners, and the next day four cars pulled up to the house. Church friends moved the books in record time.

Small Successes

Persons who receive care are keenly aware of their small successes, and these signs of success give them hope. When John first awakened from his thirteen-hour surgery, he couldn't move his legs at all. Several days later he could lift his right leg, but not his left, which John described as "dead." Surprisingly, he was able to wiggle the toes on his left foot, and this motion gave us hope. Every physical therapy session gave him hope as well.

Rehabilitation progress is measured in small increments such as a twitch, reflex, a fraction of an inch, an inch, and more. When he first learned to stand, John could only stand for a minute. Then he was able to stand for two minutes, and then three. Each minute was a triumph and sign of hope. To some, a minute may not be worth notice. To us, it was an incredible achievement, so incredible I wanted to contact the media about it.

Anesthesia took away John's sense of taste, and he had to force himself to eat. Consequently, he didn't enjoy food and ate little, which resulted in a weight loss of about forty pounds. Now that he is home again, John's sense of taste is slowly coming back, and this change is another hopeful sign. Sometimes he feels sensations in his left leg. Could the movement and function of this leg return?

You may have had small miracles of your own. A new medication prescribed for your loved one may be working. The surgery your loved one feared was successful. Your loved one may not recognize you for weeks, and suddenly say your name. Patient charts are filled with hopeful examples. Small successes like these give you energy and hope. "I love you" may be the most powerful sentence in any language.

Power of "I Love You"

Some days are "off" and do not go the way you planned. Caregiving is a constant challenge if your loved one has dementia. As an illness or a condition progresses, your loved one's behavior may change. If she or he is demented, your loved one may hit others, or steal from them. Trying to reason with your loved one can be a waste of time. Besides, arguing with a person you love is a terrible experience. Nothing you say seems to register, yet your loved one may hear three small words—"I love you."

This sentence literally changes lives. Years ago, Professor Leo F. Buscaglia of the University of Southern California taught courses on the power of love. He wrote many books on the topic, including *Love: What Life is About; Living, Loving and Learning;* and *Loving Each Other.* Many of his books became best sellers and he was often on television. I read two of his books and saw him on television several times. Buscaglia became known as a love lecturer and guest speaker, and many of his ideas may be applied to caregiving. One idea: love changes us personally and has the power to change others. Later in life, as I gained more experience (good and bad), I realized love could help one cope with despair.

I've known despair. Chances are, you have also known it. There were times when I saw only darkness and no light. A glimmer of light would appear, and then despair would pull me back into darkness. John was anesthetized for almost a month while he was in intensive care. I visited him three times a day. The nurse would cut back on his anesthesia so John would know I was there. Because he was barely awake, John's memories of this time are fuzzy, but he remembers me being at his bedside and hearing my voice. Every time I visited him, I spoke the same three sentences:

You are alive.

You are doing well.

I love you.

Most of the time, when John heard these sentences, he squeezed my hand in reply. The hand squeezes reminded me of the power of love. You may have discovered this fact yourself. While love is the foundation of your caregiving, it may also be a beacon of hope that lights your way. The most amazing thing about love is that it grows all through life. I love John more each day. You may feel the same way about your family member.

SMART STEPS

- Mentally reverse roles with your loved one, to feel what it is like on the other side.
- Respect your loved one's need for modesty and privacy.
- Know which medications affect your loved one's memory.
- Help your loved one update his or her sense of self.
- Stay in touch with family and friends.
- Celebrate small successes.
- Encourage your loved one to find a new purpose in life.
- Reap the benefits of laughter.
- Find hope in your husband or wife, in your family, in medical advances, and in religious or spiritual beliefs.

Chapter 3

Facing and Accepting Illness

SMART STEPS: P. 40

Your loved one may have been diagnosed with a severe or long-term illness, and this situation was a shock to you both. Or perhaps the diagnosis confirmed your suspicions—the scary thoughts that had been bothering you for months. You may have noticed your loved one's shortness of breath, her or his difficulty in climbing stairs, and wondered if heart disease was the cause. The diagnosis confirmed your suspicions. What will the future hold? Knowing how a health-care team works can help to quell your fears.

Health-care Team

Health-care teams are comprised of experts who work together to improve your loved one's health. These teams are also known as *patient care teams, interdisciplinary health teams,* and by several other names. A physician usually heads the team, and each member has specific duties. Team members include physicians (specialists, hospitalists, surgeons, and so forth), physician assistants, nurses, nursing assistants, technicians, pharmacists, physical therapists, occupational therapists, administrative staff, social workers, and others. During the course of an illness, your loved one may have several teams—one in the emergency room, one in surgery, one in the intensive care unit (ICU), one in rehabilitation, and one for home health care.

Remembering the names of all the team members can be a challenge. If you're upset, or confused, or don't know what to do next, ask a team member for more information. Don't be afraid to ask questions. My younger daughter came to visit her father in the ICU. She and I were invited to attend morning rounds with the health-care team. After team members had given their reports, the supervising physician asked us if we had any questions.

"Is my father going to die?" my daughter asked. The physician took a deep breath, stood up tall, looked her in the eyes and exclaimed, "Not on my watch!"

Many team members will give you their business cards. Save them all, because you may need to contact members in the future. Store the cards in a card case, or bind them together with a rubber band. Attend patient-care conferences and take notes. Follow the advice you receive at the conferences. You may have useful information to share that can help team members do their jobs. For example, your loved one may have hearing loss, and health professionals don't know this, so you can share that information.

Chronic Illness

A chronic illness is one that lasts three months or longer, according to the Centers for Disease Control and Prevention (CDC) article, "Chronic Disease and Health Promotion." The article states that chronic diseases are the leading cause of death and disability in the United States. These diseases include heart disease, stroke, arthritis, cancer, diabetes, obesity, multiple sclerosis, and respiratory illnesses. Arthritis is the most common cause of disability, the CDC notes. Smoking is also considered to be a chronic disease; this debilitating condition causes emphysema.

Caring for a person who has a chronic illness is difficult because of the progressive nature of the illness. My grandmother had severe arthritis at a time when few pain medications were available. She lived with my aunt and uncle for several years. As the years passed, however, my aunt became exhausted and asked my mother to take over as the family caregiver. So my grandmother moved in with us and lived with us until she died.

Our house was a tract house, and the rooms were small and close together. My grandmother stayed in the room that had been my brother's room, at the front of the house. At night, I could hear her moaning in pain, and her moans often kept me awake. At the time I was a senior in high school and couldn't understand why this affliction had happened to my sweet, kind, hard-working grandmother. She had done nothing to deserve such pain. I wondered if arthritis was passed from one generation to the next. Would I get it? I am a grandmother now and have two arthritic hips. I also have arthritic hands from typing (we now say keyboarding) for more than thirty-six years.

The ripple effects of chronic illness are far-reaching. Gail Sheehy, author of *Passages in Caregiving* (2010), believes that people with chronic illness battle the aftermath of medical treatment. The body becomes weak and, as illness progresses, starts to fail. Routine things like walking and eating get harder as the person reaches a middle place, which Sheehy calls the in-between stage, the time when the body starts to shut down.

Entering the hospital's ICU for the first time to visit John was an in-between experience for me, the caregiver. Before I went in, I had to wash my hands with sanitizer. The air smelled like medicine. The patients were quiet, but monitors and machines beeped constantly. John was hooked up to several machines via a spaghetti-like array of wires. While the machines were keeping him alive, he was bleeding to death internally. Health-care team members pumped blood into him as fast as he lost it, but they couldn't replace blood fast enough. John would die if surgeons didn't take action. A surgeon tried twice to stop the internal bleeding with laparoscopic surgery (through the stomach). These attempts failed, and John continued to bleed internally.

Miraculously, a retired surgeon, who was a world-renowned expert in aortic dissection, was in the hospital that day. John asked to see him. When they met, the surgeon didn't mince words. "We're going to have to open you up and clean out all the junk," he announced. John was willing to have drastic surgery because he wanted to see the twins graduate from college. They had lived with us for seven years, and, in John's mind, their graduations would mean he had crossed a finish line. In addition to getting to that milestone, he wanted to continue to be involved in the twins' lives.

John's chances of surviving the surgery were slim, and I called our minister. She came immediately and prayed with us. "In the ICU life hangs in the balance," I said, "halfway between life and death." I knew the scale of life could swing either way; John could die, or he could live. Four surgeons operated on him for thirteen successive hours. At eight o'clock in the evening, I received a phone call telling me the surgical team was "closing." John survived the surgery, and, though he couldn't attend the twins' graduations, he knew they graduated with honors. In fact, when he heard they were going to graduate with honors, John cried.

"I was willing to roll the dice," he told me later. Because John had "rolled the dice" he lived to see the twins graduate from college and get meaningful jobs. He not only lived to see our granddaughter get engaged, but he escorted her down the aisle in his wheelchair on her wedding day. When I saw John at the back of the church, my granddaughter's arm linked with his, both ready to come down the aisle, I began to cry. As the two people I loved so much came closer, I saw other people in the church were crying, too. Apparently the wedding was an emotional experience for many.

You may be in an in-between place now, and it is painful. A loved one's life may hang in the balance. Because you are in crisis, you may feel your life is hanging in the balance as well. Help is available to you. National organizations may have branches in your town. Help is available online. Talk with your loved one, and work out a care plan together. For example, you may investigate at-home care and the agencies in your community. Should your loved one have home hospice care or move to a hospice center? Questions like these need to be answered. You may also need to learn about catastrophic illness, something you never dreamed would happen to your spouse. But when it does happen, you need to know what to do.

Catastrophic Illness

Catastrophic illness is defined as a severe illness with high treatment costs. It usually requires a long hospitalization, and disability is always a possibility. This type of illness impacts all family members. Medical bills roll in ceaselessly, like ocean waves on a sandy beach. That's bad enough. Add confusing health insurance plans to the situation, and you are in trouble. What is covered, and what is not? Can you estimate your total bill? How quickly will insurance companies respond? This time is scary for both caregivers and receivers.

Work responsibilities may prevent family members from visiting their relative. Other family members may be ill. Finances may also be a problem. Not being able to visit a relative who has a catastrophic illness can cause feelings of guilt, and guilt has a tendency to build. For family members, the fear of having a disabled relative has become reality. Life has changed forever. Adapting to this change will take time and emotional spadework. You worry about your loved one and yourself. At this time, national and local health agencies, family members, and your religious/spiritual community may be sources of help.

Disability

Disability is complex. The concept means different things to different people. When people become disabled, they may not be able to walk, use their hands correctly, or control elimination. They may lack physical strength, have speech problems, or be legally blind. Caring for a disabled individual is a special challenge because things can often get worse. Your loved one's lungs may start to fail, and she or he may need to use an oxygen concentrator, which is a portable unit on wheels. Alzheimer's disease and other forms of dementia eventually cause disability.

Caring for someone with Alzheimer's is difficult because of the person's poor short-term memory and dwindling communication skills. Your loved one may misinterpret what she or he sees. She or he may perceive the color tan as blue or be afraid to walk across parking space lines. Disability forces you, the caregiver, to constantly hone your coping skills.

The entire family is affected by disability. Members of the immediate family, especially children, must learn to adjust to it. Daily schedules may have to change. Furniture may have to be rearranged. Medical equipment may have to be purchased. You may have to renovate a bathroom to meet your loved one's needs. Projects like these can mess up your home, and strain your patience and budget. A disability diagnosis can hit with hammer force.

As I was leaving the ICU, I met a nurse manager. "How is my husband doing?" I asked.

"I don't think he will walk again," he replied honestly.

His words stunned me. Though I had suspected this possibility, I had pushed this painful thought to the back of my mind. I thanked the nurse for the information, walked to the parking garage, unlocked my car, got into the driver's seat, and sobbed. I sobbed all the way home and long after I was home. I grieved not for myself, but for John. Nonetheless, I found comfort in the fact that John was alive, and I looked forward to spending more time with him. His being in a wheelchair wouldn't alter his love for me or my love for him.

Our twin grandchildren grew to know John largely as a result of tragedies. In 2007, our elder daughter (the twins' mother) died from injuries she received in a car crash. Two days later, John's father succumbed to pneumonia at the age of ninety-eight and a half. Though I anticipated his death, it still came as a shock. Two months later, my brother (and only sibling) died of a heart attack. In the fall of the same year, the twins' father died from injuries he received in another car crash. The court appointed John and me as the twins' guardians. They were fifteen and a half years old when they moved in with us. Since then, the twins have gotten to know and respect their grandfather.

While you are coming to terms with disability, keep your loved one's needs in mind. The care receiver needs her or his family and opportunities to socialize. Your loved one may develop new hobbies, support new causes, volunteer for organizations, and offer wise counsel to family members. John has replaced his father as the patriarch of the family, and members of the extended family realize this change. He continues to be, and always will be in my mind, the loving, brilliant, kind man I married.

Care Receiver's Needs

The health-care team will identify the essential needs of the person needing care, such as a wheelchair friendly home. Treatment recommendations will be made. Your loved one may be referred to community agencies that provide follow-up and home care. Caregiving is a challenge if the person receiving care is disabled, in frail health, has Alzheimer's, or another form of dementia.

Talk with your relative about his or her needs. Pick a good time for the conversation. It's best not to have this conversation when the person is in pain, sleepy because of medications, or tuckered out from physical therapy. Listen carefully and try not to interrupt. Learning about needs isn't one conversation—rather, it's an ongoing conversation. You may wish to make two lists of needs: one for you, and another for your loved one. Home care needs may include renting a hospital bed, renting a bed trapeze, opening an account with a wheelchair taxi service, ordering incontinence supplies, and arranging for physical therapy.

You and your relative have different needs. Although you both agree on some needs and are willing to discuss them, other needs may remain hidden. The idea of discussing these disagreements can make you wince. Keep in mind that changes in your loved one's health may change her or his needs. Review the list of needs, and identify the ones that require lead time. When a request is sent to Medicare, for example, it can take months to receive a reply. Your request must include written orders from a physician or another member of the health-care team, which increases lead time.

Medicare regulations can also affect when you perform certain tasks. You may order equipment from a company, only to later find the order wasn't processed. This snafu happened to me. I ordered a wheelchair for John, but weeks passed and it didn't come. I called the wheelchair vendor and discovered the order had not been processed. According to the vendor, Medicare regulations say an order for a wheelchair is processed *after* the patient has returned home, and not sooner. The first request was rejected because Medicare thought the documentation didn't support a wheelchair request. Follow-up requests from a physical therapist and the wheelchair vendor were successful, thank goodness.

Planning

Treating or caring for an ill person requires planning, and that person needs to be involved as much as possible in the planning. Where do you start? Medicare offers some suggestions in this article on its *Ask Medicare* website: "How Can You Plan for the Future?" Key planning areas include legal needs, finances, notes, records, files, and preventive care. The article points out that Medicare can reduce many expenses, but it doesn't cover everything, and some things will require significant sums of money from you.

Social workers, nurse managers, and home health-care agencies can assist with planning. To prevent confusion, stay in touch with everyone who is involved in your loved one's care. Good communication can save time. I was going to contact a physical therapist for John. However, when I attended a care conference, I learned the social worker had already made the call. It was a good thing I found out about this situation—otherwise, two therapists might have been hired for the same job.

Planning may generate more questions than answers. What is the yearly cost of care? Do other family members live nearby? How far away is the grocery store? Do you have transportation options? What are your loved one's interests and hobbies? Who should be contacted in case of emergency? Are savings sufficient to pay for home health care? These questions and others need to be addressed during the planning process. As you plan, you can learn more about sources of financial aid.

Nancy L. Mace and Peter V. Rabins, MD, examine planning in their book, *The 36-Hour Day* (1981). Friends may drift away, they point out, and making new friends is hard, especially if the spouse isn't included. Mace and Rabins think caregivers need to keep their friends and hobbies throughout a long illness, to give them support and a change of pace from the job of caregiver (pp. 35–36). I have followed their advice. Besides friendship, there's another issue to consider, and that is facing a future without your spouse. This aspect is a painful part of planning, and you can't avoid it, no matter how hard you try. Maybe the time has come to ask for help from family.

Help from Family

When a family member is ill, other family members usually rally, but they can't help you unless they know their help is needed. Stay in touch with family members, and update them regularly. Be specific about your needs. If you're getting low on groceries, for example, ask a family member to shop for you. A family member could take over caregiving for a few hours so you can grocery shop. Your religious community, health professionals, and community organizations are other sources of help. Be sure to thank those who help you.

As you make plans, you may be surprised at the amount of help that is available, especially from your family. Then, again, you may be surprised at the lack of help from family. You may feel that you do all the work, family members do nothing, and wonder why this situation is happening. One reason could be grief. Family members, including you, may be experiencing anticipatory grief, a complex and powerful feeling of loss. Anticipatory grief hurts, and some family members may distance themselves from an ill relative, to protect themselves emotionally. This reason may be, in part, why they don't help you.

Awareness of Anticipatory Grief

Anticipatory grief is a feeling of loss before a death or dreaded event occurs. You may not recognize this grief for what it is and dismiss it as a bad mood. Several factors make anticipatory grief unique. Your thoughts jump around from past to present to future, a cycle that can make you think you are going crazy. You are dealing with an incomplete and prolonged loss. If caregiving lasts for years, this loss can contribute to your exhaustion. Each day is filled with anxiety and dread, and you wonder if your loved one will die today. Anxious, sorrowful feelings are tempered with hope. Maybe someone will invent an operation or miracle drug that will save your loved one.

Days pass, caregiving continues, and suspense builds as you await the end. All this time, the symptoms of anticipatory grief are growing, and there are many:

- Denial
- Emotional numbness
- Mood swings
- Crying spells and a choked feeling in your throat

- Anger
- Depression
- Inability to concentrate
- Forgetfulness
- Vulnerable feelings
- Changes in your own health

Psychotherapist Jennifer Kay comments on this mixture of symptoms and feelings in her article, "Anticipatory Grief," posted on the *Today's Caregiver* website (www.caregiver.com). She says care receivers may grieve for the loss of their previously healthy bodies. Meantime, the caregiver may wish that this person were out of his or her misery. "Care recipients and caregivers need someone to hear and validate their feelings," Kay writes.

Mental health professionals and caregiver support groups can help you survive this difficult time. (Chapter six of the book you are reading contains more information about support groups.)

Legal Matters

You may have legal responsibilities for the person in your care. If you exercise power of attorney for your spouse, for instance, you are legally bound to protect and represent her or him. Legal duties may include paying bills, selling a house or condo, disposing of furnishings, settling debts, and other tasks.

A Durable Power of Attorney is slightly different. This document allows a person to give legal authority to someone else—in this case, to you. It also allows the designated person to make financial and legal decisions. *Durable* means the document is effective even if the other person (called the "principal") becomes demented or mentally incompetent. If your loved one has Alzheimer's, another form of dementia, or a chronic illness, you may want to get a Durable Power of Attorney now. This document will help you protect your loved one's assets, monitor his or her health care, and plan end-of-life care.

Checking your loved one's will is a wise move. Is there a will? Has a lawyer reviewed the will recently? Laws may have changed since the will was written, and it may need to be updated. Find out if your relative has a Living Will, a document that details her or his wishes in case of terminal illness or accident.

Other legal issues that can come up may surprise you. For example, your spouse, the same person who was always dependable when it came to paying bills, may have a stack of unpaid bills. Contractors who have not been paid may have filed lawsuits against you. You may close charge accounts, and your loved one may open new ones. Worse, she or he may have been defrauded of thousands of dollars. Trouble similar to these problems can happen to seriously ill, chronically ill, and demented people. Now you must clean up the mess and conserve any remaining funds— more tasks to add to your list!

Positive Self-Talk

Staying positive is difficult when you're confronted with so many non-stop challenges. Self-talk can change your outlook. An article on the Mayo Clinic's website, "Positive Thinking: Stop Negative Self-Talk to Reduce Stress," says positive thinking usually begins with self-talk. "Self-talk is the endless stream of unspoken thoughts that run through your head," the article notes. Positive thinking has many benefits. It can increase your life span and help you combat depression. When you have a positive attitude, you are more resistant to colds and feel better physically and emotionally.

The article goes on to say positive self-talk can reduce the threat of death from cardiovascular disease. But talking positively to yourself can be tricky, and you may not realize what you are telling yourself. Being aware of negative self-talk can help you control it. With practice, you may change your negative thoughts to positive ones. When a dark thought comes to mind, balance it with a bright one. Over time, this coping skill may become automatic. Smile, because smiling fosters hopeful thinking. Personal pep talks have worked for me and may work for you.

SMART STEPS

- Save the business cards you get from health-care team members, so that you can contact them later.
- Share helpful information, such as a hearing loss, with health-care team members.
- Be aware of the ripple effects of chronic illness.
- Talk with your loved one about her or his needs.
- Ask family members for help if you're falling behind.
- Watch for the symptoms of anticipatory grief.
- Ask a lawyer to review your loved one's will.
- Get Power of Attorney, if necessary.
- Say positive things to yourself.

Chapter 4

Assessing Your Loved One's Abilities

SMART STEPS: P. 53

Caregiving begins with an evaluation. This assessment may be relatively easy if the person has severe dementia. You can sense, just by being with this person, whether short-term memory is poor, word retrieval is difficult, or she or he is generally confused. But people who have memory disease can fool you for a while. One day, the person may "vegetate." The next day, much to your surprise, she or he is pretty alert. This phenomenon happened when I was my mother's caregiver, and I thought I was going crazy with such mixed signals. Health professionals can evaluate your loved one's abilities, beginning with mental alertness.

Mental Status

A physician may use the Mini-Mental State Examination (MMSE) to determine your loved one's alertness. This informal exam can be done anywhere, at your loved one's bedside, in a physician's office, or in a nursing home. The examiner asks short questions dealing with appearance, orientation, attention span, memory (recent and past) and language ability. What year is it? Which season is it? Where are you? Can you count backward from one hundred by sevens? A *MedlinePlus* article, "Mental Status Testing," reviewed and updated by Christos Ballas, MD, says these questions check thinking ability and "determine if any problems are getting better or worse."

The person may be asked to explain a well-known proverb, copy a drawing, or make an illustration from scratch. To evaluate mental ability, the person may participate in the Clock Drawing Interpretation Scale. This simple test has three steps: 1) Draw a clock. 2) Put numbers on the clock. 3) Draw hands pointing to a given time. Many variations of the test exist, according to "10 Scoring Approaches for Alzheimer's Clock Draw Test: Alzheimer's Early Detection," an article by engineer and technical support expert Michael Pekker. His article is posted on the *Alzheimer's Review* blog.

The test taker may be given a blank piece of paper or a piece of paper with a circle on it. Points are assigned for the circular shape of the clock, all the clock numbers, and correct time. The fewer points the person gets in the test, more you should worry about the symptoms of Alzheimer's disease. The article notes, "A normal score is four or five points out of five." Ill as she or he is, your loved one may be aware of mental status tests. Some health care professionals conduct an MMSE every time they see a patient. They do this because they think it is necessary or because they need information for government forms.

Health-care professionals will look at the person's chart and check the medication history. Drug interactions will also be considered. How many prescription medications is the person taking? How many over-the-counter medications is she or he taking? How long has your loved one been taking them?

The person may also be asked about pain. A person in acute pain focuses on pain and doesn't want to play word games or answer questions. That is why many health-care professionals use the Wong-Baker Faces Pain Rating Scale to evaluate pain. The patient is shown six faces that depict pain and asked to choose one that applies. Pain may also be rated on a scale of one to ten, with higher numbers indicating higher pain. Medications may be adjusted according to the pain rating.

High-tech machines may also be used to evaluate mental ability. A computerized axial tomogram (CAT scan) takes pictures of the brain. An electroencephalogram (EEG) is a test that measures changes in the brain's electrical activity and can detect dementia. A physician may also order a magnetic resonance imaging test (MRI). One of the most amazing tests, the MRI uses pictures of the brain to detect vascular abnormalities and the presence of brain tumors. An MRI can also show a person's brain in action as he or she responds to questions, solves problems, and remembers events. The test can also be used to examine how a person's brain reacts to certain drugs.

Mental status assessments may also include psychological testing. Jane Framingham, PhD, describes some of these tests in her *Psych Central* article, "What is Psychological Assessment?" To rule out the possibility of diseases, such as arthritis, this type of assessment is always done in conjunction with a physical exam, according to Framingham. Assessment components include psychological tests, interviews, observations, and informal assessment. The psychologist takes these data and weaves them into a "picture of the person being tested." This picture is then used to help health-care team members—and you—to create a care plan.

As you plan, remember that forgetfulness may be temporary. A person's mental abilities may come back slowly, so you need to be observant.

Physical Status

A physician will conduct an exam to assess the person's general health. What does a physical exam include? It will start with a medical history. Vital signs (blood pressure, heart rate, respiration rate, and temperature) are checked, along with appearance, heart, lungs, head, neck, stomach, reflexes, skin, arms, legs, and joints. Teeth, gums, nose, ears, and eyes are also checked. The physician may also check prescription medications. The exam may be shortened if the person has had a recent physical.

The health-care provider may encourage you to sign up for a website port. Many hospitals and clinics offer this service. The patient registers and provides a username and password. These safeguards will allow the patient to have online access to a number of things, such as the physician's diagnosis, a list of medications that have been prescribed, and the personalized treatment plan. Registering for a port can save you return trips to the doctor. You may also renew prescriptions on the port.

The person should have an annual physical exam. An annual exam will help you track health improvements and declines. A nurse practitioner, supervised by a physician, may perform a physical exam. Follow-up tests may be ordered. The goal is to gather as much information as possible. This information helps health-care team members, you, and your loved one to see the big, overall health picture, not just part of it. The person's treatment plan is based on this information.

Activities of Daily Living (ADL)

The Activities of Daily Living (ADL) are the ordinary, regular tasks of life, including bathing, brushing one's teeth, dressing, shaving, combing one's hair, and toileting. A person may be able to perform most of the Activities of Daily Living but have difficulty with one or two. For example, a person who has arthritis may not be able to bend over to tie shoelaces or cut toenails. If the latter is the case, you will have to do it or arrange for a podiatrist to provide this care.

An occupational therapist may do an ADL assessment. The therapist may also check the person's Instrumental Activities of Daily Living (IADL), which helps evaluate a person's ability to manage finances, drive safely, grocery shop, fix meals, use the phone, manage medications, and do housework. People with memory problems may fool caregivers for a while, but their difficulties become evident in time. Your loved one may have been a careful driver in the past, but perhaps now he or she is taking chances that make you gasp. For example, if you make a comment about your wife having "lead foot," she may become defensive. Test by test, fact by fact, a detailed picture of your loved one starts to emerge.

Another illustration of problems may be visible in an emergency-department physical. Your loved one may have had a heart attack or stroke and need to go to a hospital's emergency department. Triage is the first stop. The health-care team there will decide if the patient is in immediate danger of dying, whether his or her condition is urgent or less urgent. Team members get a brief patient history, check vital signs, and run necessary tests. Electronic records will be retrieved if your loved one has been seen there before. (However, the emergency department isn't the place to get a physical exam; rather, it is the place to get immediate help for an urgent illness.)

Communication Skills

Perhaps the person has difficulty framing sentences, retrieving words, or remembering a conversation that happened ten minutes ago. Communication skills are complex, learned skills that involve listening, speaking, delivery, and body language. Stress can block effective communication in caregiver relationships. You and your relative may both be stressed, yet unaware of just how much stress is affecting the two of you. Indeed, you may be struggling mightily to communicate with each other. The following tips will foster better communication:

Observe body language. Do you see signs of tension, such as a twitching eye or jiggling feet? Does your loved one look relaxed or tense? Does she or he participate in conversations or give curt answers to questions?

Get more information. Your loved one may think she or he has made things clear when, in truth, things are unclear. Say something like, "I'm sorry, but I didn't understand that. Can you tell me more?"

Demonstrate interest. Nod your head in agreement or interject a short comment, such as "You're right." I used to reach out and touch my mother's hand to show her I was listening.

Be patient. Forgetful people may retrieve a word that starts with the right letter of the alphabet, only to speak the wrong word. Or a person may use incomplete sentences. It's best not to point out these errors.

Summarize the conversation. A short recap helps to clarify things for both of you. Thank your loved one for any additional information she or he supplies. You may also compliment your loved one and say, "Wow! You have a good memory."

Forgetfulness

Memory problems can hinder communication or, in some cases, stop it cold. In the book *The 36-Hour Day*, Nancy L. Mace and Peter V. Rabins, MD, compare forgetfulness to entering a theater in the middle of a movie. You have no idea of what happened earlier or what is happening now. A forgetful person may not recall what happened ten minutes ago and, for no special reason, launch into a long story about something that happened a decade ago. This discrepancy isn't deliberate, Mace and Rabins point out, but rather is related to the way the brain receives and stores information. The authors list some memory aids that may help (1981, pp. 35–36):

- A large clock
- A calendar (oversized works best)
- Activities list (printed, not in cursive writing)
- Familiar objects
- Labels for cupboard drawers
- A daily routine
- Photos of family members

Some memory aids may cause problems. My mother was close to her sister, Ada, during their childhood years. After my father died, my mother impulsively moved to Florida so that she could be near Ada. Family members didn't even know she had moved. Ada was in her mid-eighties at the time, and her health was failing. Still, the sisters were glad to be living in the same town. They called each other often, went out to dinner together, and attended social events. These activities stopped after Ada was hospitalized suddenly and died. Later, my mother remembered Ada had died, but she would remember it only for a short time.

"I wonder what Ada is up to," my mother commented, looking at a photo. "I haven't heard from her in a while."

Oh dear. What should I say? I decided to tell the truth. "She died," I replied softly.

"She died?" my mother asked.

"Yes, a year ago," I answered. Mom's eyes filled with tears, and her lips trembled. The photo that used to bring her pleasure now brought her grief. With the passage of time, my mother found comfort in using Ada's rumpled, worn purse. It was an object that linked her to her beloved sister. She continued to use Ada's purse until it fell apart. You may wish to look around the house for similar linking objects that might bring comfort to your loved one and spark happy memories.

Set Some Boundaries

Boundaries are essential to quality caregiving. Long-term caregiver Peter W. Rosenberger, President of Standing With Hope, thinks boundaries can help caregivers combat isolation, loss of independence, and loss of identity. He calls these "the three I's of caregiving." He expands this point in an AARP–Kentucky blog post by Scott Wegenast (http://states. aarp.org/caregiving-are-there-boundaries/), saying that seeing a loved one suffer can make caregivers throw good sense to the wind. We aim for normal when nothing is normal. "Our emotions are involved and that usually means we have yet to discover our own powerlessness," he explains.

Add guilt, obligation, and resentment to the caregiving mix and the result is "a swirling cauldron of dysfunction," Rosenberger observes.

Without boundaries, you, as the caregiver, are at risk for poor health, depression, and a shorter lifespan. In a perfect world, caregiver and receiver would set boundaries together, but you may have to set them for your relative. What is an example of a boundary? Let's say your husband or wife is insecure and wants you home all day, every day, and this seclusion isn't working for you. Recognizing the need for social contacts, you decide to take Wednesday afternoons off and hire companion care. Good boundaries benefit both the caregiver and receiver. Adapting to change can be hard, so you may wish to set boundaries gradually.

Say Yes When You Can

Hearing the word "no" can make your loved one try something silly or dangerous. In contrast, a "yes" can encourage your loved one and helps you gain his or her cooperation. Health professionals are trained in this approach and often use distraction in gaining cooperation. Here are some comments used by professional caregivers. As the following examples show, some comments rely on distraction.

You're getting so good with your walker!

That looks like a comfy sweater.

I hear you're an expert carpenter. Where did you work? Can you tell me more about it?

You're so funny!
You'll love dinner tonight. It's your favorite, barbecued pork and baked beans.
Would you like to watch television? Your favorite program is coming on.
I've never seen anyone work as hard as you in rehab. I can't believe you're
*   standing!*
Thank you for talking with Doris. She's new here and needs a friend.
I love your sense of humor.
You have a beautiful family.

The "yes" approach helps you reinforce boundaries. Setting boundaries is easier with a good lead-in, such as "I'm worried about you falling, so I'm removing the scatter rugs from your room." Positive lead-ins show how much you care. But the time will come when you have to say no and say it strongly. "No" can be a slippery slope, and your relative may test you. Hard as it may be, you need to remain firm and stick with this reply. You're making progress and don't want to slide backward now.

Say No When You Must

Chronic, long-term illness will disrupt both your relative's life and your life. There will be times when you have to say "no" to your loved one. Framing a negative message takes patience and skill. For example, a woman who was annoyed with her caregiver said, "She didn't talk nice." Her face wore a hurt expression, and she shook her head, saying, "I can't believe it."

If your loved one has memory disease, she or he may not be able to track conversations. Your loved one may be distracted easily or get stuck on part of a conversation. Once stuck on a subject, he or she may be unable to talk about anything else. Retrieving words becomes harder, and thus the person's sentences get shorter by the day. Even if these things happen, you can still "talk nice," and the following tips show how to do it:

- **Make eye contact.** Find eye contact at the beginning of a conversation and continue to make contact.
- **Use short sentences.** A short sentence structure helps your loved one track the conversation.

- **Monitor voice pitch.** A high voice can sound alarming, and a loud voice can sound angry. So avoid those tones.
- **Watch your delivery speed.** Talking fast may come across as uncaring. Talking too slow may come across as patronizing.
- **Review points if necessary.** You can make a joke and say, "I'm not sure of what I just said, so I'm going to repeat myself."

Family members can help support "no" messages. Family members may have decided it's time for their relative to stop driving. One family member can share this decision with the receiver and another person can provide verbal support later. During the follow-up conversation, the second family member can point out some positives of the family's decision. For example, "The traffic is really heavy these days, and driving is tiring." "Not driving will lower your insurance bill." "You won't have any more big gas bills or service charges." While supportive comments like these won't always erase anger, they can dampen it and redirect your loved one's thinking.

Keep a Logbook

The day may come when you mutter to yourself, "I've got to write this down." That day may have come already, not once, but several times. Where should you keep your notes, in order to stay organized and not forget details of care? A three-ring binder is ideal because notes can be grouped by topic. You can also separate notes with tab pages and add more pages, as needed. Notes may be kept in a logbook. Free logbook forms and templates may be downloaded from websites. A logbook may be an ideal place for your notes and has advantages such as the following:

A logbook can be customized. For example, if your loved one has diabetes, you may keep a diabetes logbook. You may keep separate logbooks about physical therapy, occupational therapy, activities, or expenses.

A logbook is less work for you. Logbooks don't require long entries. In contrast, diaries require daily entries, and journals require regular, periodic entries. Entries in a diary and journal are often lengthy and detailed. Logbook entries can be much shorter.

A logbook may provide information for health professionals. The physician or physical therapist may ask you to provide information about your relative's appetite, sleeping, and Activities of Daily Living. A logbook is an ideal place to track such data.

A logbook may serve as legal protection. Because you can't predict the future, you don't know if and when you'll need this type of protection. Keeping a logbook can be a protective step, to document what you have done, and to show you haven't done anything fraudulent.

For example, a sibling may accuse you of taking money from the person receiving care. This accusation would be hurtful. Or a distant relative may contact you and lay claim to your loved one's furniture, valuables, or mementos. One of my friends told me a story about a relative who wanted his aunt's painting so badly that he went to her home and stole it. "He just took it off the wall," my friend said in disbelief. Occurrences like this happen frequently.

Date your log entries, and keep them brief. If you are keeping a logbook about your relative's physical activities, you may wish to group them, such as physical therapy, occupational therapy, walking, exercises, and so on. Don't carry logbook entries over to the next year. Put the old logbook away on the last day of the year and start a new one. Over time, if you find you're writing down the same activities, your logbook may turn into a checklist. A stretching checklist might include the heading at the top, and exercises to check off: short rubber exercise band (used for stretching), long rubber exercise band, extending left leg, extending right leg, holding leg position for two minutes, and doing wheelchair "push-ups."

Complexities of Spousal Care

Spousal caregiving can come with communication problems, conflicting feelings, and cause you to forget to take care of yourself. You may spend so much time caring for your spouse that you don't take good care of yourself. Social contacts fade away, and you may start talking to yourself, a worrisome development. Are you taking care of yourself? Now may be a good time to get a check-up, if you haven't had a physical exam in several years. The results of your exam may surprise you, such as finding out you are anemic.

Another issue that may bother you is the lack of a sexual relationship. Though you and your spouse had a good sexual relationship before, caring for a spouse who has Alzheimer's disease may include some embarrassing moments because the disease can erase inhibitions. Your spouse may bring up sexual topics at social gatherings, for example. Talk with a geriatric physician or one that specializes in Alzheimer's disease if you are concerned about your sexual relationship with your loved one.

Reversing roles with your spouse may be painful for you and your spouse. Yet, it is unavoidable. This situation may be one of those problems that require less discussion between the two of you, not more. As a caregiver, you need to do what is necessary. You may go to the bank to find out the balance in your joint savings account, the accrued interest, and ask for a print out of this information. You may pay organization dues, renew or cancel magazine subscriptions, and do other such tasks on behalf of your spouse.

Memorandum for Record

A Memorandum for Record (MFR) is an in-house record of events that wouldn't ordinarily be put in writing. Keeping such a record is common in the military. At first glance, you may think an MFR has no relationship to caregiving. Give it some thought, however, and you may find it helpful to keep an MFR. Family members may squabble over caregiving. Perhaps every time you see them, the conversations turn into arguments. A sibling may accuse you of maintaining an unsafe living environment, something to record in an MFR. Your MFR entries can ease your worries and may serve as legal protection later.

I thought I needed legal protection after a speech therapist reported me to the director of my mother's assisted living community. The speech therapist told the director that I mistreated a vulnerable adult. What really happened was that the speech therapist had called me to ask for permission to begin speech therapy with my mother. "My mother doesn't need speech therapy," I replied. "When she speaks, she speaks clearly. She has had dementia for years. What she really needs is a new brain." Fortunately, the staff of the assisted living community knew me. They didn't believe the therapist's claim, and, some months later, the speech therapist was dismissed. I wrote down these hurtful events in an MFR.

This was a bad experience, and I think of it often. You may have gone through something similar. In cases such as this one, an MFR entry could include a written account of what has happened, when it happened, and how it happened. Thus an MFR can be legal protection. You don't have to write down everything. Jot down the most important information: date, facts, quotes, your actions, and concerns. Put your MFR away for a few days, take it out, and proofread it for accuracy and brevity.

Monitor Health Changes

Changes in your relative's health may come suddenly or slowly. You notice a change and then, because you're so busy, you may forget it, and go about your day. The team professionals need to receive updates from you about changes in health. These changes may be nothing to worry about, or they may be significant and require immediate attention. Keep a list of the changes you observe. Your list may be as simple as a few words on a notepad, entries on a calendar, or checkmarks on a form downloaded from the Internet.

Which health changes should you note? Breathing problems are always a concern. A loved one with heart disease may have to stop and rest after walking a few steps. If he or she is gasping for breath, that should be noted. Symptoms of diabetes should also be noted. If your loved one has memory disease, you need to document changes and when they happened. Your notes can help the health-care team fine-tune your loved one's treatment. Assessing your loved one's abilities isn't an easy job, but it is a necessary one.

SMART STEPS

- Talk with your loved one's physician about her or his mental status.
- Accompany the person to doctors' appointments.
- Work on communication skills and listen attentively.
- Observe the person's body language.
- Be open to compromise.
- Understand that forgetfulness may be temporary. Be alert for signs of memory retrieval.
- Use memory aids to help a forgetful loved one.
- Identify linking objects that may comfort your relative.
- Keep a customized logbook.
- Write a Memorandum for Record, if you think it is necessary.
- Monitor changes in the person's health.

Chapter 5

What Skills Do You Have?

SMART STEPS: P. 66

Perhaps you have realized that caring for another person is a daunting idea, causing you to wonder if home health care is the best option for your relative. You may be concerned that you have not thought of everything. Do you have all the necessary equipment to do the job? More worrisome, do you have the energy you will need? You may also wonder whether you will have time for yourself amidst all this "busyness." Worrying as these thoughts may be, remember that nobody comes to caregiving empty-handed. You have skills, and you are capable of learning new ones. Now may be a good time to review your skills. Let's start with a look at innate talents.

Innate Talent

All of us have talents, be they large, small, or a smidgen. The dictionary defines talent as "a special natural ability or aptitude." Genes determine your innate talents; with training and practice, these talents may be nurtured and perfected. Maybe you have absolute pitch, the ability to identify and sing musical notes. You may have such a sense of style and color that it adds up to a talent for decorating. Knitting may be one of your talents, and your projects may be worthy of display in a museum. Talent can be obvious or less obvious, something others see in you only if they look carefully.

The famed German philosopher Johann Wolfgang von Goethe, an expert in many topics, once said that a genuine talent finds its way. What do talents have to do with caregiving? Talents can lead you in new directions. You may decide to use your artistic talent and decorate your loved one's room. If you play an instrument, you may play for your loved one in the afternoon. Sharing your talents can also serve to give you a much-needed break from caregiving. When you're feeling down, exercising your talents may lift your spirits and reinvigorate your energy.

The ability to make others laugh is a talent. While my husband was in rehab, I saw how one of the aides there used her talents to help patients. She approached them, patted them gently on the shoulder, and started a conversation or told a story. Within minutes, she would have the patient laughing.

When I complimented her on this ability, she was surprised. I said, "You make people laugh. That's a talent."

"Oh, I've always been able to make people laugh," she replied. "And I love doing it."

If you don't think the ability to make people laugh is a talent, talk to a professional comedian. I would venture to say every one of them views this ability as a talent and works hard to perfect it. You may be able to make people laugh. You may be a good listener. These are talents that you can use to boost your loved one's spirits and improve his or her day, every day.

Education and Experience

Your formal education or training, no matter what the field, may have equipped you with skills that will serve you in caregiving. For example, an engineering degree may help you with prioritizing. A teaching degree may help you establish a routine. A city planning degree may help you make care plans. A carpenter could build furniture or a wheelchair ramp. The longer you are a caregiver, the more ways you will find to apply your education.

Drawing on your education helps, but it doesn't make you immune to frustration, fatigue, worry, or the pain of watching someone's health decline. Here are a few examples that will demonstrate that, no matter how much education or experience you have, situations will arise in caregiving that you cannot predict or explain.

I was talking with a nurse who had helped care for her father, who had Alzheimer's disease. He was a resident of a nursing home in another part of the state. Her father had started to wander away from the nursing home. One day she received a call from the nursing home telling her that her father was missing and the police had been notified. The police searched the area around the nursing home and, when no clues turned up, widened their search. As leads developed, the search was expanded all the way to the other side of the state. Two days later, her father was found in a city hundreds of miles from the nursing home.

"Nobody knows how he got there," the daughter concluded. "I'm so glad he wasn't injured or killed."

Then there was the situation that knocked me for a loop when my mother was a resident of a senior living community. For some reason, my mother didn't get along with a fellow resident of the community and would argue and act aggressively toward her. One day she threatened to "biff" the woman. I have two college degrees and know how to research a topic. I had read dozens of books and articles about dementia and thought I was prepared for my mother's decline. I wasn't. There is no amount of research and preparation that will prepare you for the day when the kind, patient mother you've always known starts talking like a prizefighter to a fellow senior citizen. Or perhaps you've always known your relative to constantly worry, and find yourself vastly surprised that with Alzheimer's disease, your relative loses the incessant worrying.

Your education and experience are braided into caregiving. Being a caregiver changes you, though it may take a while for you to see the changes. According to an article on the *Family Caregiving* website, "Caregiving is Different for Everyone," short-term caregivers may not see themselves as caregivers, whereas "those providing care for years may see themselves and act more like a caregiver than [a] spouse or adult child." Your loved one may have Alzheimer's disease and, as it progresses, you may find yourself acting more and more like a parent to your parent. Such a role reversal can be painful. You need to keep in mind that your parent will always be your parent and you will always be her or his child.

Despite physical illness, your loved one may still function well mentally. Rather than simply saying this to caregivers, he or she may have to prove it to them. Some nurses and aides treated John as if he were demented, and this was painful for him. "It took a while, but they finally realized I was still sharp," he commented. "Once they realized this, we could work as a team." Working as a team changed John's relationship with his caregivers and some became true friends. "They were wonderful," John recalled. "A couple of them cried when I left the unit."

Physical Strength and Fitness

Caregiving requires stamina and strength. You may go up and down stairs twenty times a day, or push your loved one's wheelchair for blocks, or need to turn your loved one over in bed every two hours. These tasks can be physically challenging if you are small in stature. Your loved one may weigh significantly more than you. With experience, you gradually learn how to conserve energy and pace yourself in your caregiving duties. It's easy to see why health-care experts recommend regular physical activity for caregivers. You may or may not get regular physical activity. Indeed, there will be days you feel lucky to have any time to exercise.

Many caregivers (and you may be one of them) have their own health problems. Even with these problems, you may be able to build up your physical ability by doing stretching exercises and lifting small weights. Some physical activity is better than none at all. When it comes to physical strength and fitness, do the best you can, and try to be consistent. I used to be on a regular walking program. In fact, John and I walked together in our neighborhood. Though the program ended when John's aorta dissected, I still walked long distances in the hospital. Now that John is home, my regular walking program has ceased. Today, my physical activities include walking around each grocery store aisle three times, cleaning the house, lifting and repositioning John, and taking roll-about walks with him.

Caring for your loved one may require intense physical effort. A couple from my church invited me for dinner so that I could meet a woman whose husband had died recently. She had taken care of her husband during his long-term illness. He had used a hospital bed equipped with a trapeze.

While her husband used the trapeze to help himself change positions, she still had to lift him. "I was surprised at the arm muscles I developed," she said.

Your caregiving days may include more physical activity than you realize. There are many small ways to increase the amount of physical activity that you are capable of. Instead of stacking items at the bottom of the stairs to carry up later, make separate trips. Stretch your arms and legs while you're watching television. Walk around every aisle in the grocery store two or three times.

I can almost hear you saying, "But I don't have time to exercise." There are solutions to this problem. You may ask someone to stay with your loved one while you take a walk. You could join a health club and work out there once a week. Perhaps you could become a mall walker.

If you wish, track your physical activity in a logbook. Keeping a logbook can boost your motivation. No matter what it takes, do everything you can to be physically fit. Make a note of everything—vacuuming, washing windows, dusting furniture, weeding the garden, and mopping floors. Seeing all that you have accomplished may make you want to do more.

A Spiritual Core

As your journey gets longer, you may wonder why so much trouble has come to you. You may question your spiritual beliefs. You may wonder whether there is a God or think God is angry with you. Watching your loved one struggle makes you sad. Your feelings may be so strong that you can neither admit them, nor express them in words. Unfortunately, these thoughts and feelings don't go away. You may need to add another task to your list of tasks, and it's spelled out in capital letters: TAKE CARE OF SPIRITUAL SELF.

This task requires honesty and self-examination. How can you do it? Attending religious services may be the first thing that comes to mind. Depending on your schedule, you may attend services regularly or occasionally. Reading, watching, or listening to inspirational works can also help. Your religious community may have a lending library, and you may check out books or other media. Participating in retreats is another option. Meditation can help soothe your spirit. Ten minutes of meditation a day can change your life.

If you haven't meditated before, there are books that can get you started. You may wish to start a home library of spiritual books. Participating in a weekend retreat is a way to take care of your spiritual self. Attending an author's talk is another method to enhance your spirituality.

Caregiving support group meetings, you'll find, may focus on spirituality. Though you may disagree with some of the views expressed, the meetings might help you reflect on your situation. Another option is to join a religious community in your town.

Disease-Specific Knowledge

Disease-specific information is only a few computer clicks away. The day you heard your loved one's diagnosis, you may have contacted a national organization, such as the American Heart Association, Alzheimer's Association, American Cancer Society, American Lung Association, Arthritis Foundation, or the National Spinal Cord Injury Association, to name a few. Hundreds of disease-specific organizations have websites with free resources and information to share with you.

National health organizations usually have state and local chapters that you may contact. Some also hold conferences for health professionals and caregivers. The Minnesota-North Dakota Alzheimer's Association, for example, puts on a conference each year, and it is well attended. These conferences give caregivers and health-care professionals the chance to share information and compare notes. Many hospitals have disease-specific support groups that you can join. For more information on these, call your local hospital, public health department, or department of social services.

Three other sources that may be of help to you include the Centers for Disease Control and Prevention (CDC), www.cdc.gov, the National Health Council, www.nationalhealthcouncil.org, and the National Health Information Center (NHIC), www.health.gov/nhic. The NHIC is a referral service that links people to organizations that provide reliable health information, and much of it is disease-specific. For more material about a specific disease, you can go to the Mayo Clinic website, www.mayoclinic.org, and click on the "Diseases and Treatment" heading. University and college websites are also good sources of information. New research findings may make some information obsolete, so keep an eye out for the latest findings concerning your relative's illness.

Public libraries are troves of information. They also have computers for public use and staff members to help you. Check your library's health section for books about your loved one's disease, or ask a librarian to order books from a branch library if you can't find what you're looking for on the shelves. The Rochester Public Library, near the Mayo Clinic, has a health room staffed by a registered nurse who checks symptoms and describes treatment options. It is one of the library's most popular departments. Disease-specific knowledge helps with daily care and, in an emergency situation, can be the difference between death and life.

Problem-Solving Skills

Problem-solving is a huge part of each caregiving day. Whether you realize it or not, you are solving problems from the minute you get up in the morning until you go to bed at night. Many of your loved one's problems may be health-related. She or he may have a fever, or complain about a painful bladder. Both of these problems require a quick response. You may have to change your schedule at the last minute in order to address such situations. On-the-job training helps you hone your problem-solving abilities. You may get so good at problem-solving that the process becomes automatic.

Both the caregiver and the person receiving care need to be involved in problem-solving. If you leave anybody out, you may be facing disappointment. This story from my family illustrates the point.

John is one of three sons. The three "boys" wanted to replace their father's rickety, dented desk. Dad had used it for decades, and it was falling apart. But the biggest problem was size; the desk was too large for his studio apartment. So the "boys" started searching for a smaller desk, and they found one. They went to see Dad, summarized the situation, and asked if he would like to go and see the desk they had chosen. Dad rejected the idea immediately. "That's very kind of you, but I don't want a new desk," he said firmly. "I like my old one."

Creativity

Medical experts, scientists, and other researchers have tried for years to measure creativity. There are different kinds of creativity and this diversity makes measuring it more difficult. Generally speaking, creativity is the ability to generate ideas that are useful in solving problems, communicating feelings and ideas, and entertaining others. Mihaly Csikszentmihalyi, author of *Creativity: The Work and Lives of 91 Eminent People*, studied creative people for decades. He shares some of his findings in his article, "The Creative Personality," published on the *Psychology Today* website.

Creative people have a remarkable ability to adapt to almost any situation, according to the author. He uses the word "complexity" to describe these people. Instead of being an individual, each creative person is a "multitude." Csikszentmihalyi identified ten traits that creative people share, and this list is a study in contrasts. While creative people are energetic, they also seek solitude and rest. While creative people are smart, they are also naïve. These people combine playfulness with discipline, responsibility with irresponsibility, and imagination with fantasy.

There are more contrasts. Creative people are extroverts and introverts. They can be both humble and proud. Many are able to bypass gender roles and stereotypes. Imaginative people can be rebellious, and they can be conservative. Artistic people are often open and sensitive, so it is understandable that when they experience suffering, they may feel intense pain. Yet even sensitive artists enjoy life. Not surprisingly, they are passionate about what they do. Indeed, creative people are most happy when they're creating.

Creativity is essential to caregiving. As such, you are already tapping your own creativity. Each day, you try to balance "busyness" with restfulness. You may be adept at caregiving and naïve about health-care regulations. Some days your mind swings from reality to fantasy and back to reality again. When you're with family members, you may be an extrovert, whereas with strangers you are quiet and introverted. As far as passion goes, you are passionate about the care you provide your loved one. Creativeness can nurture you and tug you forward on your caregiving journey.

Time Management Skills

Good time management skills make caregiving easier and give you more time for yourself. You don't need a degree in business to manage time wisely. Experience will teach you plenty about how to pace yourself. When caregivers discuss time management, some tips come up again and again, and one such tip is to respect your body clock. This means doing the hardest tasks at high-energy times and doing easier tasks at your low-energy times. You need to determine when your most energetic time of the day is and how long your energy will ordinarily last.

You may be an early-morning person (I am). Or you might have peak energy in the afternoon, or be a night owl. Whichever you are, try to take advantage of your high-energy times, and use them to the fullest.

Dividing a big job into smaller jobs is another useful tip. Intimidating jobs are less overwhelming when you work with small segments of each task at a time. Many caregivers like to use a daily planner. Some use a small, spiral-bound book, whereas others prefer a large calendar to plan their days. Making "To Do" lists seems to be one thing caregivers agree on. Prioritize your list. I do this by putting the letter *A* by the most critical tasks on the list, the letter *B* by the less important tasks, and the letter *C* by those tasks that are least urgent.

Pay attention to how long it takes you to do each task. Maybe it takes an hour to help your relative bathe and dress, ten minutes to make the bed, forty-five minutes to make dinner, and so on. Knowing the lead-time you have for a task is essential to good time management. What's on the schedule for next week? What's on the schedule for next month? Keeping good records is another helpful tip. This involves small chores like sorting mail, keeping receipts, and filing medical bills and insurance papers. For chores like these, I do what I can when I can. Sometimes I get a jump on dinner by setting the table in the afternoon. Thanks to a good washing machine and dryer, I can do laundry any time.

Medicare and Medicaid regulations may influence some of your time management decisions. You must follow their regulations to be reimbursed for certain devices and medical equipment. Because I wanted to have everything ready for John when he came home, I ordered a hospital bed weeks in advance and bought sheets for it. This was not the best timing. According to Medicare regulations, a hospital bed must be delivered on the day a patient is discharged. If you have questions about how Medicare regulations may apply to your situation, talk with a physician or social worker.

Dependability

Of all the qualifications you bring to caregiving, your loved one may appreciate dependability most. Your relative counts on you to fulfill requests, do things well, and do them on time. Patience and dependability are related. If you have patience, you take the time to do a good job and are willing to wait for results. Caregivers who are patient are willing to attend training sessions and take courses about sterile technique, food safety, and medication safety.

When you are dependable, your loved one worries less and sleeps better. The home atmosphere is calm because you accomplish tasks with a smile and gentle spirit. Dependability will outshine flashiness any day, and it comes, in part, from attitude. You are dependable because you have chosen to be.

A friend of ours is going blind. New medications and surgery have slowed the progression of his blindness, but he still copes with it each day. He is very aware of all his second wife does for him and is grateful for her dependability. "I have Mary now," he said. "She takes good care of me."

Active Listener

Listening seems like a passive activity, and many times it is. However, active listening is far from passive; it requires extra effort. Dr. John Warner, author, management consultant, and coach, describes active listening in his article, "How to Listen Attentively," posted on the *Ready to Manage* website. Active listening requires you to follow certain key steps. If you don't, you will be a passive listener. Though you will be present, you will be hearing some points and missing others. You need to be an active listener to understand and recall health information. Warner says the process starts with motivation. Here is an edited list of his steps with some comments added by me:

Step 1: You have to want to listen to the explanation, conversation, or class. Wanting to listen keeps you awake and attentive. I have to listen carefully to my husband because some of his medications affect memory and he occasionally uses the wrong word.

Step 2: You have to pay close attention to the person who is speaking and bring your mind back to the present when it wanders.

Step 3: You must devote your full attention to the whole message being delivered—attitude, values, feelings, body language, and words. When you are focused on the whole message, it may surprise you.

Step 4: You should provide feedback when necessary. A one-word reply, a nod, or an affirming sound will usually serve the purpose. I often say "Got it" or use a thumbs-up gesture to show that I have listened and retained information.

Step 5: To check for accuracy, you need to paraphrase or summarize what you just heard. This step can lead to surprises because one person's summary may differ greatly from another person's summary.

Although you're an active listener, you may want to keep working on your skills, especially if you are caring for a child. Young children do not have the vocabulary to describe their feelings or pain. A teenager may hide feelings from you but share them with peer-group friends. Whether communication is spoken, written, or visual, communication skills keep everyone "in the loop" and on track.

SMART STEPS

- Apply your talents to caregiving.
- Understand that education doesn't immunize you against the pain of watching a loved one decline.
- Make physical activity part of each day.
- Take care of your spiritual self.
- Learn more about your loved one's illness.
- Have a contingency plan.
- Apply your creativity to caregiving.
- Divide big jobs into smaller jobs.
- Do what you can, when you can.
- Contact a physician or social worker for information on Medicare and Medicaid regulations.
- Choose to be a dependable caregiver.
- Work on your listening skills.

Chapter 6

What Skills Do You Need?

SMART STEPS: P. 79

Comparing the skills you have with the skills you need can be upsetting. Questions keep coming to mind. Do I have enough time to gain these skills? Will these skills really help me? What costs are involved? New skills are another task to add to your long task list.

Coping Skills

Someone may ask you, "Are you afraid?" A friend asked me this question, and it sent chills down my spine. Questions about your preparation, the health of your loved one, the number of caregiving duties you've assumed, and how much assistance you need can make you apprehensive. Then, again, so much may be happening right now that you may not have time to be afraid. If you are an experienced caregiver, you have an idea of what to expect. If caregiving is new to you, however, you may feel intimidated. Your relative may pick up on your anxiety, and, in turn, become anxious. You can prevent this from happening by following these self-care steps:

- **Get enough sleep.** When you are short on sleep, your thinking can be distorted and feelings can be magnified. Adults need seven to eight hours of sleep per night.
- **Evaluate your eating.** Food affects how your mind works. When you can eat a balanced diet, your thinking will be more efficient. A balanced diet includes the right amounts of starchy foods (potatoes, bread, rice, and pasta), plus plenty of fruit and vegetables. It is fine

to include some protein-rich foods such as meat, fish, and lentils. In addition, you should have some milk and dairy foods. Take care not to consume too much fat, salt, or sugar.

- **Monitor your snacks.** Many packaged snack foods are loaded with empty calories that provide little or no nutritional value. Instead, find a few healthy snack recipes at the library or on the computer, and try out what appeals to you.
- **Reward yourself.** Do something for yourself every day. Read a magazine, call a friend, or go to a movie.

Gary Berg, editor-in-chief of *Today's Caregiver*, believes caregivers can marshal their courage and become "fearless." In an editorial, he explains that fearless caregiving is a process, not a destination. "Once you are on your way, you will recognize how to use fear as a motivation," he explains. Fear may be a source of energy and lead to positive steps. For example, you may decide to get some more training. The training will not be easy but, in the long run, it could be worth it. In addition, what you learn might be helpful to you at work. For example, perhaps you put your apprehension aside and decide to take a computer course to learn how to set up spreadsheets to track such things as medical bill copays, insurance premiums, medications, and rehab progress. Learning how to make and use spreadsheets might also help you to get a raise or a promotion at work.

More Education

A one-day workshop, college course, or online course may just what you need. Check the Internet, and you may be amazed at the number of online courses available to you. Many state governments offer training courses. State boards on aging may have information for you. The Minnesota Board on Aging, for example, has developed a free "Caregiver Resource Guide" that includes concise fact sheets on a variety of subjects: caregiving tasks, basic planning, financial planning, self-care, getting help, and managing moves.

Local organizations, such as The Salvation Army and the YMCA, offer classes. Before signing up for a course, make sure you understand which subjects are covered and how much the course costs. Perhaps you want to learn about lifting techniques and find that this isn't part of the course. The public school system may offer an adult education course that meets your needs. The following organizations offer caregiving education:

- Family Caregiver Alliance (www.caregiver.org)
- Institute for Caregiver Education (www.caregivereducation.org)
- Alzheimer's Association (www.alz.org/index.asp)
- Family Caregivers Online (www.familycaregiversonline.net/online-education)
- Caregiver Training University (www.caregivertraininguniversity.com)
- Caregiving College (www.caregivingcollege.com)
- Medicare (www.medicare.gov)
- Rosalynn Carter Institute for Caregiving (www.rosalynncarter.org)
- American Caregiver Association (www.americancaregiverassociation.org)

Finding the right course can be time-consuming, so allow lots of lead time. You may save some time in your search by visiting www.caregivercertification.com/ and reading the article, "Google Top 5 Caregiver Education Programs." In addition to describing the programs, the article lists their pros and cons.

You may also need training in specific procedures, things like using a mechanical lift, taking blood pressure, or helping with self-catheterization. This kind of lift is used to transfer a person from a bed to a wheelchair, or from a wheelchair to a bed. The lift has two basic parts: a sling and a transfer mechanism, which is operated by a crank or electricity. The sling must be attached properly or the patient could fall. Your relative may need this type of lift after being discharged from the hospital. Nurses will be glad to show you how to safely operate a mechanical lift.

You may need to learn how to use a blood pressure cuff to measure your relative's blood pressure. An electronic cuff can take six readings in eight minutes, and this type of cuff can be set to take fewer readings. To get an accurate reading, you need to follow three steps:

1. Your relative must sit still and be quiet. This means no talking or moving of the arms or legs.
2. The person should have both feet on the floor and should not cross his or her legs.
3. If the person complains of arm pain while the cuff is getting a reading, press the stop button. Arm pain may be an indication of high blood pressure.

In order to assist a loved one who has incontinence problems, you need to learn sterile technique. You will wear medical examination gloves. There are two types, sterile and non-sterile. The latter cost less. Your relative should cleanse her or his hands with a sanitizer before working with catheterization equipment. Put hand sanitizer on non-sterile gloves before using them. The genital area should be cleansed with a sterile wipe. Output will be measured with a urinal "pitcher," and the amount recorded in a small notebook. Tracking bowel movements in the notebook is also a good idea.

With so much going on in your life, you may feel forgotten. "I don't see anybody," a caregiver commented, "and I have to change this situation." While you may agree with the point, you may not know how to reduce isolation and loneliness. One thing is for sure: You cannot, and should not, let prolonged loneliness continue. Instead of waiting for someone to rescue you, you will have to take steps to reduce isolation and loneliness and rescue yourself. As my mother used to say, "The good fairy isn't coming." She would say this to help me take responsibility for myself and become my own good fairy.

Ways to Reduce Isolation and Loneliness

Long-term caregiving is an isolating experience. Many days you don't see anyone else, just your loved one. While you may wave to a neighbor, answer a couple of e-mails from friends, or talk to them on the phone, you don't meet people face-to-face. Relatives may not contact you because they think you're doing well and don't need their help. Short-term loneliness can become prolonged loneliness, which is a hazard to your health.

"Loneliness: A Surprising Health Risk," an article in the *Mayo Clinic Health Letter* (July 2014, p. 6), details some of the harmful effects of loneliness. Research findings suggest that loneliness may increase the chances of premature death by fourteen percent. Other harmful effects include depression, fragmented sleep, and increased inflammation of the body. It may surprise you, but there is also an increased risk of developing dementia. The article goes on to point out that the concept of *loneliness* doesn't mean "being alone." When you're alone, you may be content, do things you want to do, and use the time to be productive and invest in yourself.

How can you reduce loneliness? Reaching out to others helps. Joining a caregivers' support group may be useful. Staying involved with your hobbies is another thing you can do to ward off loneliness. Even if you are tired, try to continue with some hobbies and pursue new interests. Nancy L. Mace and Peter V. Rabins, in their book *The 36-Hour Day*, say hobbies may be put on the back burner for a while, but not discontinued altogether. They go on to say hobbies will help you later in life: "When the time comes that you no longer have the care of this person, you will need friends and activities" (1981, p. 257).

This may be a good time to learn more about a new hobby, join a book club, or attend a talk at the public library. You might sign up for an adult education course. Staying in touch with your religious community also helps to reduce isolation and loneliness. Becoming a caregiver doesn't mean you have to give up your interests or identity. The opposite is true: you must keep your interests and identity in order to be a good caregiver. In short, you need to still be you.

Systems for Tracking Meds

Pharmacies sell "med minders," which are small boxes with multiple compartments. In the various marked compartments, you can store and track the daily medications your loved one takes. Med minders can cost from a couple of dollars to $45 or so for a high-tech minder that beeps when a dosage has been missed. You don't have to buy a med minder though. A simple form that lists your relative's medications and specifies dosages and when to take them will do the job. Other options include medication-tracking software and smartphone apps.

Yet another high-tech method of tracking medications has been approved by the U.S. Food and Drug Administration. Hunter Stewart tells about the invention in a December 12, 2014 *HuffPost* website article, "Pill-Tracking Device Could Monitor Whether You're Taking Your Medication." A tiny, digestible chip, the size of a grain of salt, can be inserted into pills. The patient wears a skin patch, and a sensor inside the chip sends a message to the patch that tells when the next dose is due. This device is being tested now.

Unless such high-tech aids intrigue you, you don't have to worry about salt-grain-sized chips, or various apps, or med-tracking software. The quickest solution to your med-tracking problem may be downloading a template from the Internet. Or you can do what I do. Every morning, I print out a list of John's medications and check them off as I give them to John. It is a simple system, and it works.

Compassion Fatigue Plan

Compassion fatigue is a form of physical and spiritual exhaustion. Caregivers who have this troublesome feeling describe their lives as a blur or living in a gray world. Susanne Babbel, PhD, MFT, writes about the seriousness of the condition in her *Psychology Today* article, "Compassion Fatigue: Bodily Symptoms of Empathy." Health professionals (caregivers) are affected by their patient's trauma to the point where if the patient's health suffers, the caregiver may become tired and stressed.

Your body can become weary and so can your soul. The symptoms of compassion fatigue can have an impact on your health. Here is a list of symptoms:

- **Sleep problems.** These include interrupted sleep, nightmares, and flashbacks.

- **Forgetfulness.** You find yourself doing silly things, such as putting a comb with the kitchen utensils.
- **Psychosomatic illnesses.** You may have unexplained stomachaches and muscle aches.
- **General grouchiness.** If you are rarely grouchy, you may wonder about the source of feelings of irritability.
- **Lethargy.** You feel too tired to do anything and keep postponing things.
- **Emotional numbness.** You develop an "I don't care" or "whatever" attitude.
- **Substance abuse.** This may be a way of medicating yourself, and it is harmful.

The Compassion Fatigue Awareness Project website (www. compassionfatigue.org) lists more symptoms: blaming behavior, ignoring others' feelings, compulsive behavior (such as excessive spending), preoccupation, and denial. Compassion fatigue isn't something to ignore. To get an idea of how it is affecting you, take the "Compassion Fatigue Self-Test: An Assessment" posted on the *CFAP* website. According to the instructions, there are no right or wrong answers. You respond to a list of statements with the numeral 1 for "very true," numeral 2 for "somewhat true," numeral 3 for "rarely true." If you have more than fifteen "very true" responses, it is time to review your self-care strategies.

Emergency Plan

Having a medical emergency plan is essential to quality caregiving. There are so many things to consider, that you may wonder where to start. Basic safety is a good starting point. You may stock up on things like batteries, first aid supplies, medications, and water. "I have a flashlight in every room and a supply of candles and matches in case the power fails," one caregiver shared. You might also want to use a weather radio.

Linda Burhans, author of "10 Things to Include in a Family Caregiver's Home Health Emergency Care Plan," posted on the *Harmony Health* website, approaches the topic from a health standpoint. She tells caregivers to write the plan, put it in a three-ring binder, and write "EMERGENCY CARE PLAN" in bold letters on the front. The binder should include this information:

- Name and contact information for the person who has Durable Power of Attorney
- Health insurance information
- List of prescribed medications, dosages, and dosage times
- Health testing needs, such as for diabetes and high blood pressure
- The person's food allergies
- List of drugs that shouldn't be taken together

Gathering this information takes time; but you will have it when you need it, and that will save you time and stress in the long run. I live in a tornado-prone state, and I know I must take shelter if I hear a horn warning. The laundry room is the safest place in our home. A bathroom, storeroom, or basement may be safe places for you. Stock this area with pillows, blankets, medications, water, and snacks. You may wish to practice going there with the person you are caring for.

Medical Talk

Doctors, nurses, nursing assistants, and other health-care professionals speak a specialized language, one you may not understand. For example, the primary care physician may describe a treatment plan and, as he does so, other health professionals will nod their heads in agreement. Meanwhile, you're trying to figure out the gist of the conversation. The National Library of Medicine has posted a quick guide to medical talk on its website, (www.nlm.nih.gov), "Understanding Medical Words: A Tutorial from the National Library of Medicine." You will need Flash Player to download the guide to your computer (see http://get.adobe.com/flashplayer/). These proactive steps will also help you in understanding medical lingo:

Ask questions. It is fine to query the health team with questions such as "Would you please explain that to me?" and "What does that mean?" You could also ask health-care professionals to repeat information.

Request written information. This information could be a fact sheet, brochure, or booklet. Many health centers have displays of free information for patients and families.

Ask for a diagram. Sometimes a picture is worth a thousand words. A simple drawing may clarify things in seconds.

Buy a book about medical terms. One such reference book can save you hours of time and worry. Even better, the book is on your shelf and within reach whenever you need it. Many helpful articles about medical jargon are available on the Internet. Download a few, print them out, and put them in a folder or three-ring binder. Soon, you'll be fluent in "medi-speak."

Self-Confidence, A Gift to Yourself

Self-confidence is the belief you have in yourself, your judgment, and your decisions. When it comes to some tasks—perhaps baking, getting laundry done, or speaking to your church—you are confident. Home caregiving, on the other hand, may shake your normal confidence, and you may wonder if you can do it. You wouldn't be the first home caregiver to have a lapse of self-confidence. I noted with interest that blogger Elizabeth Hanes had shared her fears in a post on *Caring.com*. It is titled, "Caregiver, Have Confidence!" She uses the words "woefully inadequate" to describe herself and says she feels insufficient as a wife, nurse, writer, woman, and caregiver. Then, after some reflection, she realized she was wasting energy on negative feelings.

"Starting today, I'm going to begin focusing on the things I do well, rather than those areas in which I'm lacking," she writes. "I urge you to do the same."

You wonder how to apply this advice to your situation. With all that's going on, you may feel that you have little time to boost self-confidence. Some examples of confidence-boosters have been cited previously, such as balancing negative thoughts with positive thoughts. Acting confident may also help boost your self-confidence; or, as a popular saying goes, "Fake it 'til you make it." Reviewing your abilities and skills may help you recharge your self-confidence.

Your self-confidence will come to the forefront as you focus on your loved one instead of yourself. Self-confidence makes your days easier and your relative more comfortable. Experience can provide a strong boost to your self-confidence. Because of experience, you have a clear idea of what you can do and what you cannot.

As time passes, lack of sleep may impair your thinking and whittle away at your self-confidence. Health-care experts recommend at least seven hours of sleep a night, preferably eight. If you are getting less sleep than that, you may need a sleep plan. After dinner I watch "light" television, such as decorating or cooking programs. Sometimes I do laundry. An hour before bedtime, I start turning off lights. I turn down the bed and put on my pajamas. I make sure all the doors are locked, so I won't worry in the middle of the night. Finally, I ask my husband if there is anything else he needs.

Better Sleep Plan

Ask caregivers about their biggest problem and many will say sleep deprivation. Lack of sleep can have many causes. You may have to give your relative medicine in the middle of the night. A loved one with Alzheimer's disease may start to wander at night. Worries may keep you awake; and once you start worrying, you keep on worrying. When you get back to sleep, it's not the restful sleep you need. Sleep deprivation affects your energy, decision-making abilities, and endurance. Without enough sleep, your energy "battery" is low.

How can you get a good night's sleep? The Mayo Clinic offers some suggestions in its website article, "Sleep Tips: 7 Steps to Better Sleep." Here is the revised list with added comments from me:

Keep regular hours. Each day, go to bed at the same time and get up at the same time. If you do this routine long enough, you will automatically wake up in the morning and not need an alarm clock.

Have a bedtime ritual. Slow down, eat a light dinner, and avoid tobacco and alcohol in the hours before retiring. Some people also avoid spicy foods later in the day. A warm bath before retiring may help you relax and fall asleep.

Get a comfortable mattress and pillow. Buy a new mattress if your mattress is decades old. You may wish to buy a "body pillow," one of those long ones that molds to the contours of your body. A mattress topper may also promote restful sleep.

Limit daytime naps. If you've been deprived of sleep several nights in a row, you may need to take a short nap. Avoid napping for several hours at a time. Instead, try to limit naps to one hour.

Make physical activity a part of each day. Being active helps to promote sleep because activity uses up energy. You may try a few exercises before you get dressed in the morning to get things rolling.

Lower stress. "Be calm" is one of those tips that is easier said than done. Joining a caregivers' support group may help you to manage stressful feelings.

Many Americans have televisions in their bedrooms. The bedroom is not the ideal place for television viewing; rather, it is a place for sleep. Though you may not realize it, television programs may put ideas into your mind that keep you awake at night or cause nightmares. Turning off the television a few hours before you go to bed is a smart idea. A slightly cool bedroom also promotes sleep, so lower the thermostat or open a window. Some people benefit from "white noise," which is background sound that fosters sleep, and they use small fans to generate this noise.

Doing something for yourself every day can promote sleep. When you go to bed, you may be less apt to think about your problems and, instead, think about what you did for yourself today. Be satisfied with the tasks you accomplished. Taking care of yourself will certainly help you sleep better. In the morning when you awaken, you will be ready and eager to start the day. You will be able to approach the day with energy and enthusiasm.

Support Group

Joining a support group can help immensely. Hospitals, national organizations, religious communities, senior centers, and nursing homes all have support groups. Choose a group that meets at a convenient time and place. A caregivers' support group may be one of the few settings where you can talk freely about caregiving and feel understood. You may relate to other caregivers' stories and benefit from other people's trial-and-error process.

Trust is another benefit of a support group. If you attend meetings regularly, over time you may develop trust in other group members and find yourself sharing more. Sharing caregiving experiences helps in validating those experiences. You should attend meetings regularly in order to reap these benefits. Some caregivers attend meetings only occasionally. Some say they do not like to share their feelings or speak in public. Lack of transportation may also be a reason for irregular attendance at meetings. If getting there is a problem for you, see whether another support group member may be willing to give you a ride.

Before you join a support group, find out who runs it, learn about the leader's qualifications, talk with some members, and ask about the rules. Is the group affiliated with a hospital, national organization, or local religious community? Group participants should feel comfortable, and every person should get a chance to speak. Confidentiality is the primary rule of all support groups. Support groups have a main premise: *What is said in the group, stays in the group.* It is a wise and considerate rule to follow.

SMART STEPS

- Recognize your fears, and take steps to deal with them.
- Take care of your own health so you can care for your loved one.
- Get more education if you think it will be helpful.
- Have a system for tracking medications.
- Create a "compassion fatigue" plan.
- Take steps to understand medical talk.
- Give yourself the gift of self-confidence.
- Learn from your mistakes and failures.
- Prepare for emergencies.
- Establish a sleep routine.
- Do something for yourself each day.
- Join a support group.

Chapter 7

Getting Ready for Home Care

SMART STEPS: P. 93

Your caregiving mosaic is almost complete, and the shards have been gathered. You've considered daily tasks, your loved one's illness, her or his abilities, your existing skills, needed skills, and additional training. Now it is time to consider some of the nuts and bolts of caregiving, beginning with the daily routine. Like the foundation of a house, your routine provides a structure for your relative and you. Try your routine for a few days, and modify it as needed. You may have to "test drive" several routines before you are satisfied.

Establish a Routine

Having a daily routine is doubly important if you rely on paid caregivers. Paid caregivers "float" and go to different houses and towns. You may get the same caregiver several days in a row, a different caregiver the next day, and a new caregiver the next week. These caregivers need to know the daily routine. Your loved one should be aware of the routine as well. Post it on the refrigerator or put a copy on the bedside table. Divide the routine into sub-routines: getting up, medications, meals, physical activity, and bedtime. Routine is essential for someone who has Alzheimer's disease. In fact, having a routine may reduce his or her agitation.

A routine can always be adapted to changing circumstances. For example, while the paid caregiver is present, you may catch up on laundry, go to the grocery, run errands, or make soup for supper.

Elizabeth Hanes writes about her routine in a *Caring.com* blog titled

"Daily Routines: Write Them Down!" As she explains, "My brain doesn't need one additional thing taking up space. Pen and paper work much better for tracking routines." This caregiver types her routines, inserts the pages in plastic page protectors, and puts them in a three-ring binder. Using plastic page protectors allows her to check off items with a dry-erase marker. What does a daily routine look like? Our routine is in the table below.

The Hodgsons' Daily Routine	
7 a.m. – 8 a.m.	Paid caregiver gets John up for the day and assists with self-catheterization. The paid caregiver also does light housekeeping tasks. I get organized for the day and do some writing.
8 a.m. – 9 a.m.	I serve John breakfast and his first round of medications. I usually go to the grocery store around 9 a.m.
9:30 a.m. – 10:30 a.m.	Physical or occupational therapist works with John. I do chores and continue writing.
11 a.m. – 12 Noon	I pay bills, do laundry, make advance preparations for dinner, and perform other housekeeping tasks.
12 Noon – 12:30 p.m.	I serve John lunch and his second round of medications. Then I take an hour nap to catch up on sleep. Sometimes I wash another load of laundry, fold laundry that's been washed, or do other chores.
3 p.m. – 3:30 p.m.	I help John with self-catheterization, go to store, work on chores, or write.

3:30 p.m. – 5 p.m.	John takes nap. I do chores and cook dinner.
5:30 p.m. – 6 p.m.	I serve John dinner and his third round of medications.
6 p.m. – 8 p.m.	We watch television, read, or engage in a planned activity, such as a "roll stroll" in the neighborhood.
8 p.m. – 10 p.m.	Paid caregiver supervises wheelchair exercises, helps with self-catheterization, and gets John ready for bed. I give John his final medications of the day.
3 a.m. – 3:30 a.m.	I help with the self-catheterization.
5 a.m. – 6 a.m.	I wake up and start another day.

I followed this routine for five months, and it was challenging. By mid-afternoon, I was yawning and yearning for sleep. When John had a return visit with a member of his rehabilitation team, she suggested moving the three a.m. self-catheterization to four a.m. This one-hour change helped me immensely. Now I can get about six hours of uninterrupted sleep and am grateful for them.

Everyone involved in your loved one's care should be aware of the routine. They don't need to know every detail, just the key times of the day. Being familiar with the daily routine helps you, your relative, and paid caregivers to plan ahead. Many caregivers need to modify their homes in order to care for a person. If your home becomes a remodeling project, your routine will be temporarily disrupted.

Modify Your Home

Safety is your top priority. Inspect your home for barriers that may pose problems or be hazardous to you and your relative. State or local agencies that are assisting you may conduct a safety check for you. The person who inspected our townhome was done in fifteen minutes and said everything was in order. You may need to clear traffic patterns, install wheelchair ramps, or add a fire alarm a few feet from each bedroom. Repairs you have postponed for months may now have to be made. Some recommended repairs may strain or exceed your budget.

Try to see your home through your loved one's eyes. Do you have steep steps? Are hand rails lacking in your staircases? "Home Modifications for People with Dementia and Barriers to Implementation," a study posted on the *Dementia Today* website, examines some common barriers. The study was conducted by Gesine Marquardt, PhD, Deidre Johnston, MB, and Ann Morrison, PhD. Study procedures were reviewed and approved by the Institutional Review Board at Johns Hopkins School of Medicine. Eighty-two households from neighborhoods in north and northwestern Baltimore, Maryland, participated in the study. While the majority of caregivers modified their homes to correct physical limitations, they often failed to address hazards such as defective railings, rickety stairs, blocked traffic patterns, lack of maneuvering space, and substandard repairs.

"Most caregivers were not aware of environmental interventions that could prevent wandering," the study notes. Does this finding apply to you and your household? For example, the Alzheimer's Association suggests keeping car keys hidden and affixing door locks out of a person's line of sight. So you could install a sliding bolt at the top of an exterior door or at the bottom. There are some handy electronic devices that can signal when a door is opened; even a bell placed above a door could work as a way to notify you that your relative was trying to get out.

Good lighting in the home is imperative. Dark hallways are bewildering and unsafe for someone with memory disease and may cause him or her to fall. The solutions to poor lighting are simple: buy more lamps, install higher wattage bulbs, and use more night lights. Magnifying lights are also available for those who enjoy needlework and crafts. Put nonskid padding under scatter rugs to prevent rugs from shifting. You may need to have the heating and cooling ducts cleaned if you live in an older home. A bathroom fan that vents to the outside is a must; fortunately, it is inexpensive. Ceiling fans are other items you may wish to consider adding to your home.

Renovating a room in your home may be on your "To Do" list. Get several estimates before you pick up a sledge hammer. Check the Internet for reviews of contractors. Visit the Better Business Bureau's website to see whether complaints have been filed against contractors you are considering. Ask neighbors and friends who have used a particular contractor if they were pleased with the work. Be sure to find out whether past jobs by a contractor were completed on time. You don't want to be living in a construction site for months on end.

How does your loved one feel about home modifications? That's an important question that he or she may have difficulty answering. Drastic changes may cause him or her to complain. Your planning and your decorating may be great, yet your relative may not like the changes. Put yourself in the other person's place. If you found yourself in a revamped home, you would feel strange for a while. This is normal. Caregivers don't adjust immediately to such situations, nor do the persons who are receiving care. So be patient.

Bathroom Safety

The bathroom can be a hazardous place for a disabled person. It's easy to slip on a wet floor when getting into the tub or to fall when getting out. Bathroom safety requires more than installing a few grab bars. First, you need to consider the person's physical abilities. Can she or he get into a bathtub? The sides of the tub may be too high. A cast iron tub usually has higher sides than an acrylic tub. Talk with a plumbing expert about tubs, acrylic showers, and the difference in their measurements.

You may wish to install a security pole next to the tub or shower. A bathtub safety rail that clips to the side of the tub is another item to consider, as is a nonskid bathtub mat. If the person is disabled, you may buy a transfer bench, shower seat, or toilet seat with support handles. Make sure you check the temperature of your water heater. Some heaters turn off automatically if the temperature gets too hot. The instructions that came with the heater will tell you how to reset the temperature. If you can't do this yourself, have a plumber do it.

Make the Best Use of Space

Lack of storage is a common problem in many homes these days. Investing in storage boxes and garage shelving is often worth the money. Many stores carry easy-to-assemble shelves. Cube storage (boxes covered in cloth or cardboard boxes) is also something to consider. The frames and cubes are sold separately. Under-bed storage—plastic boxes with lids on the top and wheels on the bottom—are another option. You can find good deals on storage solutions on the Internet but be forewarned: everything I ordered had to be assembled, and one item arrived without instructions.

Dividing a room can be a problem for home caregivers. For example, you may wish to divide a large room into two areas, a bedroom area and living room or sitting area. Though you recognize the need for a wall, you may not be able to afford to have a carpenter build it. In some cases, a folding screen, blanket, or large sheet may work as well as a wall. Waist-high bookcases may be used to divide space. The bookcases should be well-built and sturdy. Check garage sales for screens, bookcases, and sheets or quilts to use.

Using a light-colored paint on walls can make a small space look larger. On the other hand, a dark-colored wall can make a room feel cozy. Choose colors carefully because they affect mood. Blue is a calming color, for example. Though your spouse loves red, she or he may grow tired of the color in a couple of months. Neutral colors are good choices because the room's accessories may be changed easily. Large furniture is the trend today, so measure your doorways before you buy any furniture. Check consignment shops, used furniture stores, Goodwill stores, and garage sales for smaller furniture pieces. If you buy on a computer site such as Craigslist, meet the seller in a public place for the sake of safety.

Home Assessment Tools

You may think your home is suitable for caregiving, yet it may lack some essential items. A home assessment can reveal deficiencies that you have overlooked. A physician, nurse, or physical therapist can advise you on home arrangements. You may create your own assessment checklist or visit caregiving websites in order to download assessment checklists. Here are two assessment checklists that will help you get started:

Home Environmental Health and Safety Assessment Tool. This two-page checklist was developed by Allison Del Bene Davis, PhD, RN, at the University of Maryland Environmental Health Education Center. It is divided into two categories: assessment areas and Standard of Practice. The assessment areas of the checklist include home construction, heating, appliances; water, smoke and fire information; pests, air quality, diet, health equipment, and cigarette smoke.

Do-It-Yourself Home Environmental Assessment List (HEAL). This tool comes from the *Clean Air for Kids Program* in Tacoma, Washington. It is ten pages long and contains two parts, a survey and an action plan. The survey asks questions about your building, nearby environment, dust and lead control, moisture, indoor air, and hazardous products. After you finish the survey, you create your own action plan.

Identify the top priority items. What needs to be fixed first? Do you need to buy anything? How much will these things cost? In the interests of better temperature control and energy savings, you may decide to replace your old thermostat with a computerized one or buy insulated shades to keep your home warmer at night. While these costs may be unplanned expenses, they can save you money in the months to come. Lower priority items on your repair list can wait until later.

Paid Caregivers

Home health-care agencies are springing up all across the country, and your community may have several of them. When shopping for these services, start with the agency's website. Please understand that registered nurses (RNs) and aides abide by different Medicare regulations. Aides cannot give injections, oxygen, or do anything with a feeding tube. Aides cannot prepare medications, but aides can hand medicine to a person. John's paid caregivers are allowed to bandage a moist wound, but not an open one.

I called most of the caregiver agencies in Rochester, Minnesota. Their hourly rates were a few dollars apart, depending on whether I hired RNs, who cost more per hour than other caregivers. I wanted help for four hours a day and chose the agency with the lowest hourly rate. Researching outside caregivers was an educational experience for me. Answer these questions before you contract with an outside agency:

Does the agency have an hourly minimum? Some local agencies had a two-hour minimum for daily caregivers. Other agencies had a three-hour minimum for occasional caregivers. You may be able to negotiate a lower rate if you contract for daily help.

Are you hiring RNs, aides, or caregivers trained by the agency? Qualifications make a huge difference in the cost of the services. Think about this point carefully because you may later be able to take over some of the duties initially performed by paid caregivers.

What is the hourly rate for an RN? Though the cost difference between an RN and aide may be small, the amount you may save can add up to a significant sum over time.

What is the hourly rate for an aide? An aide may be all the paid outside help you need. You will have to decide what will work best for your relative. The agency I contracted with asked for $1,000 up-front. This deposit is returned at the termination of services. A deposit like this can put a dent in your budget.

How often are you billed? Some caregiving agencies bill monthly, and others bill bimonthly. Keep all receipts, and file them in a safe place.

When is the deadline date? The bill should state when payment is due and whether there is a charge for late payments. The agency we work with asks for payment within two weeks.

How does the agency handle changes in schedule? You may have to notify the agency twenty-four hours ahead of time to change your schedule. If a caregiver fails to show up, call the agency and ask that this time be deducted from your bill.

Paid caregivers may be required to keep notes in a client log. They may also be asked to check things off a printed list of duties. These duties may include helping with Activities of Daily Living (ADL), light cleaning, making a grocery list, preparing meals, caring for plants, playing games, doing laundry, changing linens, dusting, vacuuming, and cleaning the toilet and bathtub.

Grocery Shopping and Preparing Meals

Caregiving tasks may limit your trips to the grocery store. A family member or friend may be able to stay with your relative while you shop for groceries. Or you may elect to buy groceries from a delivery-truck service. When you sign up, you can arrange for weekly delivery. Many grocery stores offer a shopping and delivery service to customers. To find out whether a store offers such a service, call the store or visit the store's website. You may also be able to sign up for newsletters, download coupons, and, depending on the store, chat live with a store employee on the website.

Online grocery shopping is easy. You e-mail your shopping list to the store. A staff person selects the items from the shelves and bags them. The groceries are then delivered to your home for a fee. US Grocery, Netgrocer, Safeway, Peapod, and Amazon are some of the online shopping services you may want to consider. Call your local supermarket for more information. You may also get more information on the Internet.

Try to prepare nutritious, balanced meals for your loved one. According to the *Help Guide* site's "Eating Well as You Age," by Jeanne Segal, PhD, and Gina Kemp, MA, nutritious meals feed body, mind, and soul. Good meals also provide energy and make a person look and feel better. When preparing food for your relative, consider that a person who cannot walk needs less food than someone who is walking daily. Along the same line, caloric needs change as we age. A woman who is fifty years old (or older), who isn't active, needs about 1,600 calories a day. If she is somewhat active, this number rises to 1,800 calories a day. For someone who is very active the number rises to 2,000 calories a day. In general, men need more calories than women. A man who isn't physically active needs about 2,000 calories a day, and, if he is very active, the number rises to between 2,400–2,800. These guidelines come from the National Institute of Aging website (www.nia.nih.gov).

A huge plate of food can be intimidating to some people. Smaller plates and smaller servings may make food more appealing to your loved one. Colorful meals are also more appetizing. Serve meals that include different colors, such as orange carrots, green Italian beans, yellow corn, and sweet red peppers. For more information about healthful eating, visit the National Institute on Aging website. They have informative articles, · such as "What's on Your Plate?"

Remove the salt shaker from the dining table and buy low-sodium foods. In order to continue to get enough iodine, make sure that your meals include seafood, dairy, eggs, and enriched grain products. Include "good fats," such as olive oil, salmon, avocados, and walnuts. Fiber can help lower the risk of heart disease, stroke, and diabetes, so add fiber to meals whenever possible. Whole grains, fruits, vegetables, and beans are all sources of fiber. Be wary of breads that claim to be whole wheat. A wrapper that claims the bread is whole wheat should list it as the first or second ingredient.

Hydration is essential to good health. Your relative should drink eight glasses of water a day. As we age, we are less able to differentiate thirst from hunger. A *WebMD* article, "Nutrition for Seniors: A Caregiving Primer," expands on this point. "Some older people may not feel thirsty until they are almost dehydrated," the article notes. Dehydration is a dangerous condition. Symptoms of dehydration include thirst, dark urine, dry eyes, dry skin, headache, constipation, dizziness, and lightheadedness.

The Transportation Issue

Transportation is an ongoing problem for many caregivers when they do not have a reliable car. If a relative is disabled, the caregiver may rely on wheelchair van services for transportation, and these can cost a lot in the long run. Car dealerships in your area may sell used wheelchair vans. You may also be able to rent a wheelchair van for a day trip. Call several dealerships and ask about rental rates.

Your loved one may talk about trips she or he may wish to take—a road trip across the United States, or a Caribbean cruise. While it's fun to fantasize, you may wince when you hear these unrealistic wishes. Still, travel may be doable even if your loved one uses a wheelchair. If you travel by air, you will need to reserve an aisle seat with arm rests that go up. You will also need to order a wheelchair and arrange for boarding assistance. An Amtrak train trip or bus tour are travel alternatives to consider. The local senior center may participate in bus tours for older adults, and the fees are usually reasonable. Plus, your loved one and you will enjoy the safety of traveling with a group.

Mobile Services

Your relative may not be able to go to the beauty salon or barber shop, and you will have to arrange for in-home, also known as "mobile," services. Mobile services may include manicures, pedicures, haircuts, facials, and massage. The shop may charge its regular fee for a haircut, plus an extra fee for in-home service. Choose a convenient place in the house for the haircut, and keep towels, a broom, and a dustpan handy. A haircut can lift your loved one's spirits and provide a welcome change in the day.

While a haircut may be optional, foot care is a necessity. There may be reasons why your loved one cannot care for her or his feet. Arthritis may prevent the person from bending over. If she or he is diabetic, nail problems may develop. Incorrectly cut toenails can cause ingrown toenails and infection. Be sure to cut toenails straight across; do not round the edges. Poor circulation can also lead to foot problems. To prevent skin problems from developing on the feet, the person's feet should be washed daily, especially between the toes, with mild soap or a soap that contains lotion. After a bath or shower, lotion may be applied to the feet. Make sure your relative is wearing shoes that fit properly. You may prefer to hire a podiatrist for some of the person's foot care needs. Home health-care agencies may also provide in-home foot care.

A Different Life

You might have hoped that your life could stay the same. But the truth is, life changed the minute you decided to be a caregiver. Like dust creeping under a closed window, change creeps into your life. As hard as you try, you can't keep it out. Changes in life have a way of making some things disappear. I was chatting with an outside caregiver the other day. She looked around the kitchen and commented, "I see you have a lot of cookbooks. What do you like best about cooking?"

"Everything," I answered. "I used to be a made-from-scratch cook. Those days are gone. Now I barely have time to get a meal on the table."

Carol Bradley Bursack is a speaker and caregiver. She describes caregiving realities in "Facing Reality: Caregiving Has Changed Your Life," posted on the *Aging Care* website (www.agingcare.com). Caregivers, she says, jump into their new roles with full hearts and the best of intentions. But children who are still at home have to adapt to caregiving, and this change means "getting less of you." Your retirement plans—and life plans—may have changed. Lack of time and stress can contribute to resentful feelings. Bursack asks caregivers to find some balance in their lives. "If you go years being eaten up with resentment, your own health will suffer," she writes. Take care of yourself and follow the Smart Steps on the next page.

SMART STEPS

- Establish a daily routine, and post it in a central place.
- Modify your home to suit caregiving requirements and your loved one's wishes.
- Make sure home traffic patterns are well lit.
- Take advantage of space-saving products.
- Do an assessment of your home.
- Determine whether you need the help of an RN or an aide.
- Hire caregivers from a home health-care agency.
- Subscribe to a home-delivery grocery service.
- Take the salt shaker off the dining table, and get your iodine requirement in other ways.
- Hire a wheelchair transfer service, if necessary.
- Arrange for mobile services for things like haircuts, manicures, and foot care.
- Accept the fact that life is different now and you are creating a "new normal."

Chapter 8

Caregiving Nuts and Bolts

SMART STEPS: P. 104

Ordering medical equipment is an unavoidable reality in caregiving, so this chapter is a "nuts and bolts" how-to on acquiring equipment and supplies.

First of all, find out what Medicare covers before you purchase anything. Also, get some advice on key words to use on Medicare forms. A nurse-manager told me filling out these forms was a nightmare. "We spend hours on getting the wording right," she told me. "If it isn't right, our request is rejected."

Which equipment is essential to the care of your relative? Should you rent or buy? Can you get by with less? Some items of health-care equipment, such as a mechanical lift, can take up a lot of space. Before you know it, your relative's room looks like a hospital room! You may be able to avoid this unappealing view by trying different furniture arrangements and storing health-care equipment out of sight. Can you remove some furniture? Even if you have not ever employed an interior designer before, you may wish to use one now. Two hours of professional advice can do a lot to make a room more homey.

Durable Medical Equipment

Your loved one may need durable equipment. What is meant by the term "durable" medical equipment, and does Medicare pay for it? Answers are available in a Medicare booklet, "Medicare Coverage of Durable

Medical Equipment and Other Devices." To download a copy, please go to www.medicare.gov/Publications/Pubs/pdf/11045.pdf.

The U.S. Department of Health & Human Services defines *durable* equipment as *reusable* equipment. Ordering and paying for this equipment can be a complicated process. If you have Medicare Part B, your primary care physician, nurse practitioner, clinical nurse, or physical therapist must write a prescription for the equipment. In addition, your health-care professional may have to fill out a "Certificate of Medical Necessity."

According to the booklet, "Generally, you pay 20% of the Medicare-approved amount after you pay your Medicare Part B deductible for the year. Medicare pays the other 80%." Make sure the vendor accepts Medicare payments before you buy any durable equipment. The Medicare booklet contains a chart listing equipment covered by Medicare. Here are some examples of durable medical equipment:

- Electric wheelchair
- Folding wheelchair
- Commode chairs
- Crutches
- Hospital bed
- Suction pumps
- Ventilators
- Oxygen equipment
- Walkers
- Breast prostheses
- Special shoes for those who have diabetes
- Contact lenses
- Colostomy supplies

If you own durable medical equipment, Medicare will pay for repairs and parts. Medicare will pay for repairs and parts if you are renting equipment, but payment depends the kind of equipment you are renting, which brings you back to regulations. Renting to buy is the usual practice.

Seek help from a physician, nurse manager, or social worker because the Medicare maze is difficult to navigate. Even with help, you may become confused.

Grab Bars

You may need to install grab bars in your bathroom. Buy sturdy bars that can support your relative's weight. Grab bars come in several sizes. A store or vendor should be able to give you a choice of finishes—polished chrome, brushed nickel, or bronze. If you're handy around the house and have the right tools, you can install grab bars yourself. To be sure, grab bars must be screwed into wall studs. If they are not, they could come loose and cause the person to fall.

Make sure the grab bar is within easy reach if the person uses a shower wheelchair. The easiest way to do this is to have your relative wheel into the bathroom, and then determine the position for the bar or bars. Your relative may want a couple of bars in the shower, one at the shower entrance, and one by the toilet. She or he may also ask for a toilet seat with side railings.

Walkers and Crutches

Buying a walker can be similar to buying a car, in that there are many models, many colors, and many styles. Your relative's physician will be able to recommend a walker. Still, you should try to give your loved one some choices, such as color, or a bag to hang on the walker. Before you go shopping, assess the person's mobility. You also need to consider body weight. If the person weighs 300 pounds, she or he will need a heavy-duty walker. There are different types of walkers, such as standard, folding, and seat. Your loved one may also benefit from walker accessories, such as a narrow basket, wide basket, drink holder, or storage pouch.

Crutches have to fit the person's height and needs. Perhaps the person needs an "auxiliary crutch," the most common kind (made of wood or aluminum). Hold the crutch against the side of your loved one's body, under the arm. See if the top of the crutch is a couple of inches below the armpit. Instead of buying crutches, you may rent them from a drug store. However, the store may carry only one type. A medical supply store will have several types of crutches for you to choose from.

Rolling Tables

In the middle of the night and at various times during the day, your loved one will reach for tissues, a cell phone, or the television remote. This is where a rolling table can come in handy. There are two basic kinds of rolling tables: over-the-bed tables and food trays. Check the casters before you buy a rolling table. The casters should move easily and not mark the floor. Some over-the-bed tables have a tilt feature. Discount and "big box" stores should have demonstration tables for you to examine. These tips will help you find the best rolling table for your situation:

Measure under-the-bed space. When buying an over-the-bed table, take this measurement with you when you go to the store, or have it by your computer when you search the Internet. Make sure the wheels will go under the person's bed.

Find out how much weight a food tray can support. The tray should be able to support twenty-five pounds.

Check to see if the food tray casters lock in place. This feature prevents the rolling tray or table from rolling when you don't want it to roll.

Look at the design of the legs. It's best to avoid a rolling table or tray that has U-shaped legs that stick way out, because the legs can trip you.

Check the materials. Look for a rolling table or tray that is stain-resistant and has sturdy legs of chrome-plated steel.

Compare prices. Search the Internet for medical-supply websites. You may be able to find sales, discounts, or deals that include free shipping.

Transfer Boards

A transfer board is a piece of wood or plastic that a person uses to slide from bed to wheelchair, wheelchair to bed, or from wheelchair to car seat and back again. Transfer boards can be straight, rounded, or have flaps. I have found that transfer boards sold by medical supply stores or websites cost more than those sold by drug stores. The type of board you choose depends on the person's physical condition and needs. The surface of the board should be smooth and not catch on clothing. More important, the board should support your loved one's weight. A board with a cut-out space for a handle is easier to use. In the end, price may determine the choice you make.

Here are notes on five transfer boards you may want to consider:

Basic board: This wooden board has a hand hole in the middle or toward the end. John's board is longer than some and has tapered ends for easy removal.

Tapered board: This lightweight wooden board has a wide end and a narrow end. The wide end goes on a soft surface, such as a wheelchair cushion. The narrow end goes under the person's thigh. The tear-shaped design helps to distribute the user's weight.

Beasy™ board: This board has a sliding disc that supports the user's weight; therefore, no lifting is required. The manufacturer makes three models: the Trans, TransII, and Glyder, for bathroom and bed transfers. According to the manufacturer, all of the boards support weights of up to 400 pounds.

SafetySure® board: This board is made of flexible plastic and comes in two sizes, 23-inch and 3-inch. Slide tapes allow the board to stay in place while the person slides.

SafetySure® butterfly board: Because this board is lightweight and flexible, it requires less effort from the patient. Part of the board is raised, which makes the person feel more secure during the transfer and eliminates pinching.

The Right Wheelchair

Wheelchairs may all seem the same in your mind. But wheelchairs vary, and finding the right one takes time and effort. A wheelchair needs to fit the person's height and body measurements. Armrests need to be the proper length and in the right places for your loved one to shift positions. If the headrest isn't positioned correctly, it can harm a person. The same is true of the chair cushion. An inflatable cushion may be the way to go. Wheelchairs are pricey. Some electric wheelchairs can cost as much as $33,000 or more. Medicare will help pay for a wheelchair if it is prescribed by a physician or physical therapist.

Health professionals in a *seating clinic* will make recommendations about the kind of chair your loved one needs. Staff members will measure the person's arms and legs. They will also measure the pressure points of the seat on the body. John rented a manual wheelchair for months. It was evaluated at a seating clinic, and the results were surprising. It turns out the chair was too high, the armrests were too short, the neck brace position was harmful, and the wheels were positioned incorrectly. Seating clinic personnel recommended an electric wheelchair with two large wheels (one on the left, one on the right) centered beneath his body. This is the chair he uses today.

Some types of wheelchairs that are available include lightweight models, many of which have aluminum frames, heavy-duty seats, handbrakes, padded armrests, and detachable footrests. Though lightweight models weigh about twenty-four pounds, these chairs can hold a 250-pound person. They fold up easily and will fit into a car. Transport chairs have smaller wheels and cannot be self-propelled. If you use one for a person, you will have to push it. A mobile wheelchair has a fabric back and seat and is intended for short-term use only. Some wheelchairs are equipped with a back pocket for storage.

Grabbers and Leg Lifts

A grabber is a tool that is used to pick up hard-to-reach objects. It can spare a person a lot of reaching and getting up to retrieve things. Grabbers have squeeze-type handles on one end and v-shaped grabbing blades on the other end. To grab an object, you position the grabbing blades near it and squeeze the handle. Some grabbers can be purchased for $10 or less. Grabbers come in several sizes, and you may wish to buy a long one and a short one.

A leg lift is a metal rod with a loop at each end. One loop serves as the handle, and the other loop is the one for the foot. To use the lift, a person puts the loop around a foot and hoists the leg into position. Get a leg lift with a rigid handle and loop. The loop should hold its shape and not flop around.

Be wary of ordering a leg lift that you cannot try out or examine first. As great as the product description might read, you may receive a leg lift with a wobbly handle and loop that makes the lift unusable. The fabric covering on the rod and loop may fray over time, and at this point you may want to buy a new leg lift.

Incontinence Supplies

If your loved one is incontinent, you will need more than diapers. You will also need protective gloves, nonalcoholic wipes, paper pads to protect the mattress, and trash bags. Incontinence supplies are made specifically for men and women. Diapers (also known as briefs, pads, or nappies) come in different sizes, and your relative may have to try more than one size to get a proper fit.

If you use the word "diaper" when referring to these items, your loved one may feel demeaned. "That word doesn't bother me," John admitted, "but it bothers some people." When you shop for diapers, either online or in a store, look for "adult incontinence products."

Paper underpads help protect the bottom sheet on a bed from getting soiled. Some underpads have peel-off squares that "glue" the pad to the sheet. Scented trash bags are good things to have. You never want to run out of these items, so buy them in bulk. Websites that cater to older adults have regular delivery options that should serve your purposes very well.

Other incontinence products you may need include adult panties, briefs, and plastic pants. According to "Urinary Incontinence Products for Men," an article on *WebMD*, the diaper choice depends on medical symptoms. "Lots of men hate the idea of using incontinence products," the article says, "but if you're having a problem with male incontinence, these products really can help." A male may especially appreciate a product called a "drip collector." This is an absorbent, padded sheath that goes around the penis. A plastic urinal is another useful item you may want to get. Over time, adult diapers may irritate a person's skin. Consult a physician if your loved one develops a rash or welts.

Room Monitor

A room monitor enables you to hear your loved one from another room, so that you know when help is needed. Room monitors are available for prices ranging from $43 to $200. Similar to walkie-talkies, these monitors have two parts: a sender that transmits sounds and a receiver that receives the sounds. A monitor should have a back-up power source in case the power fails. We use a monitor for John's room. Once, in the middle of the night, I was awakened by the sound of a laugh track, coming over the monitor, from a television show that John was watching. It was an odd experience, to say the least.

Consumer Reports published an article that may help you, called "Baby Monitor Buying Guide." To prevent a monitor from picking up signals from electronic devices—cordless phones, game consoles, laptop computers, notebooks, and Bluetooth devices—it recommends a monitor that has Digital Enhanced Cordless Telecommunications technology (DECT). "If you're concerned about interference, buy a digital or DECT model that's not on the same frequency band as other wireless products in your home," the article advises. You may also want to look into getting a video monitor. A room monitor can go a long way in easing some worries that you and your loved one might have.

These are just some of the caregiving supplies you may need. A well-stocked bathroom cabinet is the last "bolt." Appendix B contains a list of medicine cabinet supplies. It is a basic list. You will probably need additional supplies if your loved one is recovering from surgery, has a chronic disease, or is disabled. Your primary health-care provider will be able to give you a complete list of your loved one's medications. Keep the list in the cabinet, on your smartphone, and on a card in your wallet.

Best Equipment: A Cheerful Attitude

Caregiving is a big, complex job that can sap your energy and lead to self-doubt. Adopting a cheerful attitude can help prevent discouragement.

You don't need self-doubt. This is a time to be confident, to trust your abilities and judgment, and to smile. You are caring for a person you love, and that alone should prompt a smile. Think about the happy times you have had together, the stories you have shared, and the things you have learned together. Look for laughter in each day, and smile even when you don't feel like it.

Paula Spencer Scott discusses attitude in her article, "Wish You Could find a More Positive Attitude? My Dad's Last Lessons," posted on *www. Caring.com*. She shares things she has learned from caregiving and some of her thoughts may help you. Four of her lessons:

It is usually later in life than you think.
Doctors have lots of knowledge, but they do not know everything.
As we age, it is okay to measure quality of life differently.
Try harder to just be in the moment.

Think about things you have learned, and make a list of your own. To lift your spirits you may wish to recite or read caregiving prayers. There are many from which you may choose on the Internet. Print out a prayer, and post it where you can see it. I gave a copy of a caregiver's prayer to the paid caregiver who comes most often, and she really appreciated it. Poet, author, and children's author Jill Eisnaugle wrote "Caregiver's Prayer," a poem you may wish to read. You can find it at www.authorsden.com/visit/viewpoetry.asp?id=215935. In the poem, Eisnaugle asks for beautiful memories to bring laughter and peace to a loved one's day.

Reading poems about caregiving can help bring you a sense of peace. I love to read Robert Frost's poems. You may wish to write your own poems and prayers, either on the computer or in a notebook. Sometimes I put a poem on the refrigerator where I can see it and read it often. These Smart Steps may also lift your spirits:

SMART STEPS

- Do what you can to make your loved one's bedroom look less like a hospital room and more like home.
- Order the durable equipment you need.
- Position and install grab bars correctly.
- Choose a walker that meets your loved one's needs.
- Choose crutches that fit your relative's height.
- Measure the under-bed space before you buy a rolling table.
- Buy a sturdy transfer board.
- Check with health-care professionals before you order a wheelchair.
- Buy grabbers and a leg lift for the person, if necessary.
- Don't run out of incontinence supplies.
- For peace of mind, buy a room monitor.
- Maintain a cheerful, positive attitude.

Chapter 9

The Many Rewards of Caregiving

SMART STEPS: P. 116

Your caregiving mosaic is almost complete. You have gathered the shards—a job description, a task list, disease-specific information, physical and emotional assessments, evaluation skills, extra training, needed equipment and supplies—and are piecing them together. While you are doing this, you may ask, "Is all of this work worth it?" Time will answer this question, and the answer will probably be "yes." Indeed, you may be pleasantly surprised at the rewards you reap. Becoming John's caregiver has reminded me regularly of how much I love him.

My husband is one of the most courageous people I have ever known. He has quiet courage, the kind that may be missed unless you get to know him. When you get to know him, however, his courage becomes apparent. One of his nurses, a man facing serious surgery himself, said to John, "I hope to have your courage." John and I are a caregiving team, and his courage has made us a better team. After all we have experienced, we have a greater appreciation of family. Siblings, spouses, cousins, and second cousins have come to our aid. Every moment with family is special for us. Most importantly, we are grateful for the miracle of life.

The Miracle of Life

Your loved one may have had a near-death experience or may be a home-hospice patient, two situations that will remind you of the miracle of life. The fact that your loved one is alive may be seen as miraculous. Katrina Kenison writes about her days in *The Gift of an Ordinary Day: A*

Mother's Memoir. She tells how she slowed the pace of her life, gathered the ordinary days of winter in her mind, and strung them together like a necklace of pearls. According to Kenison, the ordinary days of life "are the only days we have" (2009, p. 264).

While you are going about your ordinary day, helping with the tasks of daily living, doing the laundry, preparing meals, dispensing medicine, running errands, remember that this day will never come again. You and your loved one have this time together. Make the most of every ordinary day; for when your caregiving days are over, these days will come to mind and you will find new meaning in them. Small events, such as a family picnic, will become more important to you, and as time passes, memories of your ordinary days may be a source of comfort.

Memories of ordinary days flooded my mind after the twins graduated from college and moved into their own apartments. I had gotten used to having teenagers in the house and watched with joy as they matured. They are grown now, on their own, and letting go has been difficult. Then I smile and think about the ordinary days and experiences we shared: gymnastics meets, choir concerts, band concerts, school plays, and fixing lemon chicken for dinner, one of their favorite meals. Ordinary events like these, plus the love and guidance they received from their parents, helped make the twins the fantastic adults they are today.

Happiness has come from sadness, and I have been blessed to be the twins' grandmother and co-guardian. I am doubly blessed to have spent thousands of ordinary days with them. You can understand why John and I shed a few tears when we talk about our grandkids. The twins continue to come for Sunday dinners, stay in contact with us, and do many things for us. If I have a computer problem, I ask my "techie" grandkids for help.

Less Institutionalization

A loved one who has been hospitalized for a long time may become institutionalized. According to the *Online Medical Dictionary* (www. online-medical-dictionary.org), institutionalization happens to patients who have been hospitalized for weeks, months, or even a year. These patients become dependent on the institution and hospital routines, and they lose the motivation to be independent. Watch for the symptoms of institutionalization, reduce them if you can, and redirect your loved one. Here are the symptoms:

Feeling cut off from the world. Months in a hospital or nursing home can make your loved one feel out of touch. She or he may not have any interest in family or things like local and global news, because these elements of the world seem like too much trouble.

Simple experiences are overwhelming. Activities of daily living, such as taking a shower, may tire your loved one and—again—seem like too much trouble. This can be hard on you.

Over-reliance on structure. Your relative may wait for cues from others before taking action. She or he may keep asking questions or giving you orders.

Sensory overload. Loud music, a television that is left on for hours on end, and beeping life-support machines may upset your relative. Constant visits from doctors and nurses may also be upsetting.

Dependence on caregivers. Dependence on caregivers can lead to uncomfortable feelings for both your loved one and you. Dependence may become yet another symptom of illness.

Subservient behavior. This behavior may surprise you, especially if your loved one was strongly independent in the past.

Treating family like hospital staff. Your relative may give you orders, or keep telling you to do things you were just about to do. For example, you may have poured coffee for both of you, but before you have a chance to turn around, your loved one asks for cream. This can be annoying.

Passivity. Your relative may not be interested in reading, or watching television, or conversation. Just as it took weeks for him or her to adjust to hospitalization, it will take weeks to adjust to being home.

Institutionalization isn't anyone's fault; it is simply what happens during the treatment of illness and recovery from illness. Someone who has been hospitalized for a long time, unconsciously or consciously, adapts in order to feel comfortable and secure. This is normal behavior, and your loved one deserves credit for adaptation. Time passes very slowly in the hospital, yet this slow time is surprisingly precious to a patient. Despite pain, hospital routines, and the constant comings and goings of staff, your relative may be thrilled to be alive. Indeed, your relative may be amazed that she or he *is* alive.

Preciousness of Time

Caregiving days are full. Some days are too full, and you may be exhausted when you finally get into bed. You may be so exhausted that you have trouble falling asleep. When you do get to sleep, it is a light sleep. Worries may make you "practice" getting up. I set the alarm at night and wake up an hour earlier than the alarm because I know it will beep. In the morning, I feel like I haven't slept at all. You may feel the same way, yet you are grateful for the time you have with your loved one.

Time is more precious and has many rewards. Caregiving may make you happy. The Dalai Lama has written several books on happiness and has made many memorable statements on the subject. You can find some of them in "50 Dalai Lama Quotes to Enrich Your Life," posted on the *Quotes and Smiles* website. One quote is especially applicable to caregiving: "Happiness is not something ready-made," he says. "It comes from your own actions."

In other words, we each create our own happiness. I was scrolling through Facebook postings and came across a saying posted by a yoga studio. Though I don't remember the studio, I remember the post: *Happiness is an inside job.* Even if your loved one is dying, it is possible to savor the miracle of life. Diana B. Denholm, PhD, LMHC, writes about the end-of-life time in *The Caregiving Wife's Handbook.* She says a slow dying process is the time for serious discussion—the last time to raise thorny issues. "And more importantly, these may be the words we have to live with," she notes (2012, p. 56). Caregiver and receiver need to have mutual respect, compassion, and kindness for one another, according to Denholm. You may have discovered the wisdom of this recommendation.

Becoming your loved one's caregiver gives you chances to get to know him or her better. Caregiving can make an "iffy" relationship stronger. You may forge a deep bond with your relative, a bond that will sustain you later in life. Many caregivers see their efforts as opportunities to "give back." You may have become a caregiver to give back to the parents who paid for your college education. Perhaps a parent gave you money when you needed it, and caregiving is a chance for you to give back. Giving back is a rewarding experience for caregiver and receiver. Better yet, it gives you chances to learn from your loved one.

Learning from Your Loved One

Learning is life-long, and many learning opportunities are built into caregiving. You may hear family stories, receive sage advice, and learn facts you didn't know before. Visiting his grandfather in the hospital's ICU proved to be a life-changing experience for my grandson. John's ICU psychosis continued for a long time. Sometimes his memories were clear, but most of the time they were a mishmash of events, a blending of reality and fantasy. Despite his mental confusion, John was determined to make things right. "We have to get the bums out!" he exclaimed once. We did not know which "bums" he was referring to, but could tell John had strong feelings about them.

"I never knew Grandpa was such a fighter," my grandson said. "I will always remember this." Young John's comment touched me, and I shared it with John. He looked surprised, and his eyes filled with tears.

You have already learned things from your loved one if you are a long-term caregiver. Perhaps you've heard about your loved one's challenges, scary life experiences, or travels. Caregiving may lead you to a new appreciation of your loved one's knowledge and wisdom. Learning more about your loved one's personality may touch your heart. "My mother was always a sweet person," a friend of mine commented. "My mother was even sweeter as she failed." Learning experiences can come at odd times, and you may wish to record them in a journal so that you can ponder them later.

Caregiving may have allowed you to learn more about your family's history. You may have learned about the tribulations family members faced when they came to America. Looking at family photos and reminiscing with your loved one may also bring forth new information. As you learn more, you may be able to identify traits passed down through the generations. Previous generations contributed to making you the person you are today. Though decades have passed, you may come to feel closer to your ancestors.

Mindfulness

Mindfulness is in vogue these days. There are societies, websites, and written materials that delve into it. What is it? Mindfulness is the awareness of what you are feeling and sensing each moment. When you are mindful, you ignore random thoughts and focus your feelings and senses on what is happening, a process some call "living in the moment." While you may understand the concept of mindfulness, practicing it can be difficult. The article, "Mindfulness Exercises: How to Get Started," posted on the Mayo Clinic website, may help you. Mindfulness can help to reduce your stress and improve your mood, according to the Mayo Clinic.

Another Mayo Clinic article, "The Path to Mindfulness and Gratitude," posted on the *Living with Cancer* blog, tells how to get started on mindful living. When you wake up in the morning, think of three positives in your life—people, opportunities, or circumstances. People may come to mind first. Remember how you felt when you were with these people. You may also recall a fond memory and "send a silent thank you [to these people] for being part of your life." Now think of ways you might show these people your gratitude. Even if the person has died, there are things you can do to express the gratitude you feel.

The mindfulness concept may be applied to caregiving. Start with the feelings you have as you perform daily tasks. You may have to fight back tears if your loved one has Alzheimer's disease. I had to fight back tears while I was curling my mother's hair with a curling iron. Looking in the mirror, my mother said, "I look old on the outside, but I feel young on the inside." Experiences like these can be poignant and may help you generate more compassion and self-compassion. You can become better attuned to yourself.

Self-Compassion

Kristin Neff, PhD, has researched and written extensively about self-compassion, which, she points out, is different from self-esteem. In a YouTube video, "The Space between Self-Esteem and Self-Compassion," she says the problem with self-esteem is how we get it. When we cultivate our self-esteem, we tell ourselves we have to feel special or above average. We can go to extremes, to the point of bullying, and focus on ourselves to the point of becoming narcissistic. Neff says narcissism has risen sharply in American culture. "Self-esteem is contingent upon success," she summarizes. If we're not successful, we beat ourselves up psychologically.

This is where self-compassion comes in. According to Neff, self-compassion has three components: self-kindness, common humanity, and mindfulness. When you practice self-compassion, you are patient and gentle with yourself. You avoid negative self-talk and any silent messages that demean you. When you are self-compassionate, you realize you aren't perfect, life isn't perfect, and, therefore, your caregiving isn't perfect. Rather than criticizing your caregiving, you savor the experience and accept it for what it is.

Maturing is a gradual process and so is self-compassion. It can take months to come to a realization. You discover something, think about it for a while, examine angles, consider pros and cons, and, if you accept it, the discovery becomes part of you.

Neff practices self-compassion and says research findings support its tenets. She thinks we're fortunate to be mammals who can be comforted with warmth, a gentle touch, and soft vocalizations—qualities that are parts of caregiving. A self-compassionate person asks, "What can I do to help?" Instead of dwelling on caregiving failures, a self-compassionate person focuses on successes. I have tried to be more self-compassionate in recent months, and it is a journey of its own. Here are some of my self-compassionate ideas:

- Putting freshly laundered sheets on my husband's bed makes me feel good.

- Cooking for John brings me joy, and this joy increases when I share meal times with him.
- Today was a day filled with problems, and, frustrated as I was, I didn't project my feelings on John or anyone else.
- My sweet, loving husband keeps thanking me for my care, and that makes me love him even more.
- It has taken me months to realize caregiving is my new mission in life, and it is sacred to me.

John thinks I am hard on myself, and he is probably right. If you, too, are hard on yourself, make developing self-compassion a goal. It is a skill worth developing, and you are worthy of it. Work on self-compassion, and practice it every day. Be persistent and, as time passes, exercising self-compassion will get easier.

Caregiving as a Spiritual Experience

Watching a loved one struggle, endure pain, or dwindle slowly is one of life's most painful experiences. One of my friends, a grandmother in her eighties, started to wonder how much longer she would live. Her wondering was due to her age, not to any problem she was having with quality of life. Her quality of life was excellent. Her husband was alive and healthy. They lived in an assisted living community and enjoyed regular contact with friends. Two grandchildren kept her busy, and she always enjoyed being with them. "I wondered why God let me live so long," she confided to me. The answer to this question became clear after her daughter was diagnosed with an incurable form of cancer.

"Now I realize I was supposed to live longer so I can take care of my daughter until she dies," my friend said. That is exactly what happened. My friend felt this time in her life was sacred.

At this time of your life, you may start to ask why questions: Why are these things happening to me? Why am I so anxious? Why am I feeling depressed? Life happens, and there may be no reason why. Dealing with spiritual issues requires an open attitude and some personal work. You may read other caregiving resources or post on a caregiving blog. Speaking to a religious leader may help you. Attending religious services may give you a spiritual infusion. One of the best things you can do for yourself is to find meaning in caregiving. Talking with other family caregivers about their religious and spiritual beliefs may also be helpful.

Letting Go

Letting go (of what you do not need, cannot keep, or lose) doesn't happen all at once. It is a deliberate, gradual evolution that involves some questions. Caregiving presents many situations in which letting go may be necessary. Debra Taitel asks three questions related to letting go in her *Daily Muse* article, "Letting Go Is a Process, Not an Event." Here are her questions, slightly revised by me:

- Would you hold onto something that was causing you great pain? If so, why?
- If you hold onto something long enough, will it turn out the way you want? What will you do if it doesn't?
- How do you fill up the emptiness in your life? How can you deal with loss? It is helpful in these situations to learn more about the needs of your community, because sometimes "giving back" can fill up our emptiness with a wonderful learning experience. Perhaps, for example, your area needs volunteers for Meals on Wheels or someone to read to the blind and you can serve a role there.

"All letting go is a process of cause and effect," Taitel explains. You need to get to the roots of your feelings. I had this thought when I was writing a book of affirmations for the bereaved. After each affirmation, I included the root of the thought, which I called the focus. One of the affirmations I wrote says, "Happiness is a personal choice." Below the affirmation, I listed the focus word, *choice*. Caregivers can choose to let go.

Taitel often sees women who stay in a miserable relationship and don't let go. "In the process of letting go, give yourself time to grieve," she advises. Think about the things you need to let go of, and how you may do it. For example, you may have to let go of the idea that your loved one will regain full health. You may have to let go of the idea that the person will live several years longer. Letting go can be a painful process. After you think it through, you may realize that letting go is easier when you do not fight it.

Each of us has to find our own ways to let go. This process requires honesty and introspection. Clearly, you cannot control every aspect of life and have to let go of some things. As you make your way, you will probably feel frustration, resentment, anger, and hope. Some feelings will be stronger than others. Ask yourself, "What do I want?" and work toward that outcome. I had to get back to basics: love for my husband, love for my children, love for my grandchildren, and love for my extended family. These basics helped me let go of things I did not need.

Gratification and Gratefulness

Letting go can lead to a new gratefulness for life. Nothing can replace the feeling of doing something good for a loved one. As you begin to love your relative or spouse in new ways, your gratification builds. Gratification is a pleasant, satisfying feeling that comes from reaching a goal. Helping a disabled person is your goal, and it is getting done. This is an achievement you may remember for the rest of your life. Indeed, caregiving may transform you.

Katrina Kenison describes transformation beautifully in her book, *The Gift of an Ordinary Day*. There were times in her life that were so difficult, she wanted to give up. But she didn't. Instead, she kept trudging on, and it paid off. She writes, "When we focus on what is good and beautiful in someone, whether or not we think they 'deserve' it, the good and beautiful are strengthened merely by the light of our attention. When we choose to see and appreciate what is good and beautiful . . . goodness can't help but grow" (2009, p. 169).

Your caregiving efforts and the efforts of other caregivers across the nation could change how we treat older adults in our country. Dr. Linda P. Fried, Dean and DeLamar Professor at Columbia University's Mailman School of Public Health, describes a new future in her article, "Older, Healthier—and Happier" (*The Wall Street Journal*, July 8, 2014). She begins by saying thirty years have been added to the average American lifespan, and, unfortunately, older Americans are asked to contribute little. "And that's what must change," she declares. Fried sees a future where older adults are healthy, connected to others, and contributing to a lasting legacy. According to Fried, older adults need reassuring roles and want to leave their children and grandchildren in good shape.

Her comment refers to older adults, but the same could be said of any person who has physical challenges. Family caregiving can help shape the future that Fried describes. Years from now, you may look back and be grateful for your caregiver role. You may grow in ways that enrich your life. The little things you do each day reflect your feelings and character. Or, as playwright Oscar Wilde put it, "The aim of life is self-development. To realize one's nature perfectly—that is what each of us is here for" (www.quotationspage.com/quotes?Oscar_Wilde).

Being a caregiver may help you actualize your true nature. The more you give in your caregiving, the more you will receive. You are a caregiver and proud of it. So share your knowledge. Talk about caregiving. Write about your experiences. Start a support group. Each day of caregiving is love in action.

SMART STEPS

- Enjoy all the ordinary days of life.
- Be on the lookout for symptoms of institutionalization.
- Make respect part of each caregiving day.
- Approach caregiving as a chance to give back to your loved one.
- Record things you've learned from your relative in a journal.
- Reduce your stress by living mindfully.
- Treat yourself kindly and with compassion.
- View caregiving as a spiritual experience.
- Remember that letting go is a process and takes time.
- Share your experiences with other caregivers, and listen attentively to their experiences.
- Be grateful for the chance to be a caregiver.

Afterword

Writing this guide has been a satisfying experience. I discovered new things about caregiving and about myself. One of the most important things I discovered is that caregiving is a complex, evolving field. As more people become family caregivers, the demand for caregiving resources has increased. Rushing to meet this demand are the U.S. government, national organizations, affiliate organizations, health publishers, self-help publishers, church groups, and online support communities. So many resources are available to you. Which resources should you choose?

One of your jobs—and it really is a job—is to find resources that mesh with your caregiving needs. I have tried to make finding those resources easier for you with this guide.

Whether it's face-to-face, online, or in a support group, interacting with other caregivers is one of the best things you can do for yourself. Joining a caregiving support group can be very helpful. Some caregivers have a false idea of how a support group works. A caregivers' support group isn't a contest. It does not operate on a "my job is harder than yours" mentality. Rather, it provides ongoing opportunities for you to share information with others, learn from others, and find solutions to your problems. Before you judge a support group, you need to attend several group meetings.

I joined a support group at my church and attend as often as possible. Though I cannot attend every Sunday, I have benefited greatly from the sessions I did attend. Those sessions helped me see that caregivers face similar issues. One person in the group sent me a handmade card with a touching message inside. I also joined the Family Caregiver Alliance (FCA). Its mission is to provide caregivers with education, services, and advocacy. According to its "About" page (www.caregiver.org/about-fca), "FCA is first and foremost a public voice for caregivers."

Routine is important in caregiving, and John and I established our routine easily. Yet there are built-in challenges to deal with, such as my lack of sleep. The buzz of the alarm clock at three in the morning was a shock. One day I purposely left the bed unmade. A few hours later, I crawled in, snuggled under the quilt, and took a nap. All in all, however, the routine we have is working well, and John and I have adapted to our new lives.

John has accepted his leg paralysis. People constantly ask, "How are you?"

"I'm good," he answers. "I just can't walk." Naturally, John has days when he yearns to go fly fishing, resume our walking program, or do ordinary things, like grocery shopping, or visiting a discount store. Then he thinks about his blessings, and how I rushed him to the hospital on the fateful evening in October 2013 when his aorta dissected. We often talk about our search for wheelchair-accessible housing, which has been a discouraging experience, to say the least.

I visited most of the assisted-living communities in Rochester, Minnesota, and I kept encountering barriers. One community had a 500-square-foot apartment available, which was too cramped a space for someone in a wheelchair. Another community had a 700-square-foot apartment available. However, the bathroom sink wasn't wheelchair accessible, and we would have had to pay for modifications to make it accessible. Though this community had health back-up services for its residents, I was told that I would have to hire outside health-care services. Another community had a vacant two-bedroom apartment, but I worried about its narrow hallways, dated decor, and lack of elevators. When I added up the extra costs, I realized building a wheelchair-friendly townhome would be cheaper. So that is what I did.

Three minutes' distance from our former home, I found a townhome that was finished on the outside and studs on the inside—no walls, doorways, or cabinets. The builder offered to move the studs and widen the doorways for free, a life-changing offer that made me weep. I tried to make the townhome as wheelchair-friendly as possible, with a roll-in shower, shower wheelchair, a microwave at waist height, low-positioned light switches John could reach, and aluminum ramps on doorways. Now, John can roll outdoors and connect with nature. Family members and friends think our townhome looks like us, and we love it. We take roll-about walks in the neighborhood and are only minutes away from downtown.

The townhome has proven to be the ideal housing solution for us. Neither John nor I were ready for a senior-living community or a high-rise apartment. Townhome living has enabled us to retain our independence. When John was in the ICU, I told him our goal was to celebrate our next anniversary. On August 10, 2014, we celebrated fifty-seven years together. "Caregiving works because of love," John said, and he is right. I am honored to be his wife, his helpmate, and his caregiver.

Home Safety Checklist

HEALTH

_____ Buy or assemble a first aid kit.

_____ Store medications in a safe place. If your relative has dementia, store medications in a locked cabinet or drawer.

_____ Dispose of all expired medications.

_____ Post the Poison Control Center phone number,

1-800-222-1222, on the refrigerator. This number will link you with the local center.

_____ Discard all dated and spoiled food.

_____ If your loved one has dementia, hide the car keys.

_____ Get an emergency call button or monitor for your relative.

_____ If your loved one has late-stage Alzheimer's, get him or her an identification bracelet.

_____ Put nonskid mats under scatter rugs, or remove rugs altogether.

_____ Keep walking areas clear and free of clutter.

_____ Keep stairs clear at all times. Do not put items on stairs to carry to the next level later.

_____ Illuminate walking areas with night lights.

_____ Tuck electrical cords under or behind furniture.

_____ Designate "parking spaces" for the wheelchair, walker, or crutches.

_____ Save the name and phone number of the primary care physician in your cell phone.

_____ Find a trusted family member, friend, or neighbor who could help out in an emergency.

_____ "Rent to own" a hospital bed with a trapeze if the person receiving care is disabled.

HOME

_____ Follow local codes and buy more smoke detectors if necessary.

_____ Install carbon monoxide detectors.

_____ Keep a fire extinguisher handy.

_____ Keep your cell phone charged.

_____ Register for a home alarm service.

_____ Add a storm door with a lock.

_____ If your loved one has memory disease, put stop signs on exit doors.

_____ If your loved one has memory disease, put safety locks on cabinets.

_____ Put deadbolt locks on doors.

_____ Make sure all doors are locked at night.

_____ Replace burned out bulbs on outdoor and indoor lights.

_____ Buy a weather-alert radio.

_____ Reinforce shaky stair railings.

_____ Rearrange furniture so a wheelchair can get by easily.

_____ Keep a small amount of cash on hand.

_____ Lock sharp knives and scissors in a cabinet or drawer.

_____ Buy a transfer bench for the bathtub.

_____ Install a raised seat on the toilet.

Appendix B

Medicine Cabinet Supplies

- Over-the-counter pain reliever
- Low-dose aspirin (81 mg.)
- Regular aspirin
- Antacid tablets
- Prescribed medications
- Large and small band aids
- Gauze bandages (roller and square)
- Paper bandage tape (hurts less when removed)
- Elastic bandage
- Hand lotion
- Body lotion
- Sunscreen
- Anti-itch cream
- Alcohol
- Antiseptic wipes
- Over-the-counter diarrhea medicine
- Over-the-counter laxative
- Cough medicine
- Cough drops
- Dental floss
- Vitamins if prescribed

- Artificial tears
- Thermometer
- Tweezers
- Scissors
- Hearing aid batteries

Note: If you have room, store prescribed medications and over-the-counter medications on separate shelves. Label each shelf.

Appendix C

Terms to Know

active listening – Paying close attention to words, attitudes, values, feelings, and body language while someone is speaking.

ADL – An abbreviation for *activities of daily living*. Includes personal care activities such as bathing, dressing, shaving, combing hair, and toileting.

anticipatory grief – A feeling of loss before a death or dreaded event occurs.

assisted living – A senior-living arrangement that may include a variety of support services and back-up health-care service.

caregiving assessment – A checklist of points pertaining to the person receiving care and the caregiver, which is used in evaluating future care.

catastrophic illness – A severe illness with high treatment costs that usually require a long hospitalization. A resultant disability is always a possibility.

CAT scan – An abbreviation for *Computerized Axial Tomogram*. This is a medical test in which pictures are taken of the brain.

Certificate of Medical Necessity – A Medicare application for durable medical equipment.

chronic illness – An illness that lasts three months or longer.

compassion fatigue – A form of exhaustion or general weariness, which can be caused by caregiving; also commonly called burnout.

dementia – A severe mental impairment and loss of personality that affects a person's ability to think clearly, recall, solve problems, and plan.

disability – A lack of physical strength, power, or mental ability that prevents a person from living a normal life or performing a specific job.

durable medical equipment – Reusable medical equipment used in health care.

EEG – An abbreviation for electroencephalogram. This is a medical test that measures changes in a brain's electrical activity.

exercise bands – Stretchy plastic strips patients use to exercise.

family caregiver – A relative who helps care for a loved one, usually without pay; this may or may not be in-home care.

grabber – A tool used by a disabled person to reach for things; grabbers come in different lengths.

half-life – The time it takes for a medication in the body to lose one half of its initial potency.

health-care team – A group of health-care professionals who work together to improve a patient's health.

home health aide – An aide who has had a short training period (six months to a year) in medical/health procedures; this aide does not need to have a high school or college diploma.

hospitalist – A licensed physician who specializes in treating patients in the hospital.

innate talent – A talent present at birth; also referred to as natural ability or aptitude.

institutionalization – A person's psychological adaptation to long-term hospitalization.

Instrumental Activities of Daily Living (IADL) – A person's ability to manage finances, drive a car, use the phone, manage medications, do housework, and other similar tasks.

leg lift – A tool that a disabled person uses to reposition his or her legs and/or feet.

licensed practical nurse (LPN) – An LPN has had training in basic medical techniques; an LPN's training usually lasts a year.

linking object – A physical object that reminds someone of a deceased loved one or friend.

logbook – A concise, written record of mileage, expenses, or specific tasks.

LPN-RN – abbreviation for *licensed practical nurse-registered nurse* (RN).

mechanical lift – A machine that is used to raise and then transfer a patient from one place to another.

mental status test – A brief or extensive test used to determine how well someone is thinking and processing information.

MFR – An abbreviation for *Memorandum for Record*. This is an in-house record of events that would not ordinarily be put in writing.

mindfulness – An awareness of what you are feeling and sensing each moment, without being judgmental.

mobile services – In-home personal care services for someone who is unable to leave his or her home.

nursing home – A facility that houses and caters to patients and provides medical and temporary rehabilitation services.

nurse practitioner (NP) – An advanced registered nurse who has taken additional courses and is licensed to write prescriptions under the supervision of a physician.

patient advocate – An intermediary who represents a patient while working with hospitals and health-care staff.

peddler – Exercise machine with two pedals that can be used with hands or feet.

professional caregiver – A person who is paid by an agency or an individual to assist in caregiving.

registered nurse (RN) – A person who has earned a college degree and who has passed a certification exam.

seating clinic – Checks the fit of a wheelchair before it is ordered and recommends changes afterward.

self-compassion – An act of being patient and kind to yourself.

self-concept – How a person sees herself or himself, and behaves, based on this perception.

self-talk – The endless stream of unspoken thoughts that run through a person's mind.

support group – A gathering of people with similar experiences, interests, and needs; some caregiving groups may be disease-specific or condition-specific.

transfer board – A sliding board used by a person to slide from bed to wheelchair, wheelchair to bed, or from wheelchair to car.

Bibliography

AARP. "10 Ways to Deal with Caregiver Stress." http://www.aarp.org/relationships/caregiving/info-06-2010/crc-10-caregiver-stress-managment-tips.html (accessed January 20, 2015).

American Eastern Institute, LLC. "Google Top 5 Caregiver Education Programs." *Caregiver Certification*. http://www.caregivercertification.com/ (accessed January 20, 2015).

Babbel, Susanne, PhD, MFT. "Compassion Fatigue: Bodily Symptoms of Empathy." *Psychology Today*. http://www.psychologytoday.com/blog/somatic-psychology/201207/compassion-fatigue (accessed January 20, 2015).

Ballas, Christos, MD; Editor/Reviewer. "Mental Status Testing." *Medline Plus*. http://www.nlm.nih.gov/medlineplus/ency/article/003326.htm (accessed January 20, 2015).

Berg, Gary, Editor-in-Chief. <1> "Caregiver Emergency Plan." *Today's Caregiver*. www.caregiver.com/editorials/caregiver_emergency_plan.htm (accessed January 20, 2015).

Berg, Gary, Editor-in-Chief. <2> Editorial on *Today's Caregiver*. www.caregiver.com/editorials/the_fear_factor.htm (accessed January 20, 2015).

Beron, Luci. "Rewards of Caregiving." North Carolina State University. www.extension.org/pages/9324/rewards-of-caregiving (accessed January 20, 2015).

Bronson, Po and Ashley Merryman. "The Creativity Crisis." *Newsweek*. http://www.newsweek.com/creativity-crisis-74665 (accessed January 20, 2015).

Burhans, Linda. "10 Things to Include in a Family Caregiver's Home Health Emergency Care Plan." *Harmony Home Health*. http://harmonyhh.com/home-health-care/ (accessed January 21, 2015).

Bursack, Carol Bradley. <1> "Facing Reality: Caregiving Has Changed Your Life." *Aging Care.* www.agingcare.com/Articles/deal-with-caregiving-changing-your-life-139977.htm (accessed January 21, 2015).

Bursack, Carol Bradley. <2> "In Caregiving, Anxiety can be Contagious." *Aging Care.* http://agingcare.com/Articles/caregiver-anxiety-stress-contagious-156605.htm (accessed January 21, 2015).

Caregiver Action Network. "Caregiving Statistics." http://caregiveraction.org/statistics/ (accessed January 21, 2015).

"Caregiving Is Especially Complicated When the Patient Is Your Spouse." *Washington Post online.* http://www.washingtonpost.com/national/health-science/caregiving-is-especially-complicated-when-the-patient-is-your-spouse/2013/01/14/fe462f80-1edb-11e2-9cd5-b55c38388962_story.html (accessed January 21, 2015).

Centers for Disease Control and Prevention. <1> "Chronic Disease and Health Promotion." http://www.cdc.gov/chronicdisease/overview/index.htm (accessed January 21, 2015).

Centers for Disease Control and Prevention. <2> "Depression Is Not a Normal Part of Growing Older." http://cdc.gov/aging/mentalhealth/depression.htm (accessed January 21, 2015).

Clean Air for Kids Partnership. "Do-It-Yourself Home Environmental Assessment List." https://www.tpchd.org/files/library/0aa73e5da1c29d0f.pdf (accessed January 21, 2015).

Compassion Fatigue Awareness Project. "Compassion Fatigue Self-Test: An Assessment." http://www.compassionfatigue.org/pages/cfassessment.html (accessed January 21, 2015).

Consumer Reports. "Baby Monitor Buying Guide." Consumers Union of the United States. http://www.consumerreports.org/cro/baby-monitors/buying-guide.htm (accessed January 21, 2015).

Csikszentmihalyi, Mihaly. "The Creative Personality." *Psychology Today.* http://www.psychologytoday.com/articles/199607/the-creative-personality (accessed January 21, 2015).

Dalai Lama. "50 Dalai Lama Quotes to Enrich Your Life." *Quotes and Smiles.* http://quotesnsmiles.com/quotes/50-dalai-lama-quotes/ (accessed January 21, 2015).

Davis, Allison Del Bene, PhD, RN. "Home Environmental Health and Safety Assessment Tool." University of Maryland Environmental Health Education Center. http://theluminaryproject.org/downloads/Tools%20-%20 HomeEnvironmentalHealthandSafetyAssessmentTool.pdf (accessed January 21, 2015).

Denholm, Diana B., PhD, LMHC. <1> "Are Your Caregiving Worries Harming Your Relationships?" *Psychology Today.* http://www.psychologytoday.com/blog/ the-caregivers-handbook/201207/are-your-caregiving-worries-harming-your-relationships (accessed January 21, 2015).

Denholm, Diana B., PhD, LMHC. <2> *The Caregiving Wife's Handbook: Caring for Your Seriously Ill Husband, Caring for Yourself.* Berkeley, CA: Hunter House, 2012, pp. 56, 142–143.

Eisnaugle, Jill. "Caregiver's Prayer." www.authorsden.com/visit/viewpoetry. asp?id=215935 (accessed January 21, 2015).

Eldercare Locator. "Adult Day Care." http://www.eldercare.gov/ELDERCARE. NET/Public/Resources/Factsheets?Adult_Day_C (accessed January 21, 2015).

Family Caregiver Alliance. "Selected Caregiver Statistics." http://www.caregiver. org/caregiver/jsp/content_node.jsp?nodeid=439 (accessed January 21, 2015).

Family Caregiving. "Caregiving is Different for Everyone." http://www.extension. org/pages/9355/caregiving-is-different-for-everyone (accessed January 21, 2015).

Fogel, Alan, PhD. "What is Body Sense?" *Psychology Today.* www.psychologytoday. com/blog/body-sense/200907/what-is-body-sense (accessed January 21, 2015).

For Dummies. "Decoding Medical Lingo." John Wiley & Sons, Inc. http://www. dummies.com/how-to/content/decoding-medical-lingo.html (accessed January 21, 2015).

Framingham, Jane, PhD. "What Is Psychological Assessment?" *Psych Central.* http://psychcentral.com/lib/what-is-psychological-assessment/0005890 (accessed January 21, 2015).

Fried, Linda P. "Older, Healthier—and Happier." *The Wall Street Journal*, July 8, 2014, p. R14.

Gandel, Cathie. "The New Face of Caregiving." *AARP Bulletin*, January 2009. http://www.aarp.org/relationships/caregiving/info-01-2009/the_new_face_of_caregiving.html (accessed January 24, 2015).

Hanes, Elizabeth. <1> "Caregiver, Have Confidence!" *Caring.com*, The Cheerful Caregiver section. https://www.caring.com/blogs/the-cheerful-caregiver/caregiver-have-confidence (accessed January 21, 2015).

Hanes, Elizabeth. <2> "Daily Routines: Write Them Down!" *Caring.com*, The Cheerful Caregiver section. https://www.caring.com/blogs/the-cheerful-caregiver/daily-routines-write-them-down (accessed January 22, 2015).

Health in Aging. "Eldercare at Home: Caregiving." http://www.healthinaging.org/resources/resource:eldercare-at-home-caregiving/ (accessed January 21, 2015).

Help Guide. <1> "Caregiving Support and Help: Tips for Making Family Caregiving Easier." http://www.helpguide.org/elder/caring_for_caregivers.htm (accessed January 21, 2015).

Help Guide. <2> "Preventing Caregiver Burnout." http://www.helpguide.org/articles/stress/caregiving-stress-and-burnout.htm (accessed January 21, 2015).

Home Advisor. "Adult Day Care Programs and Costs." http://www.homeadvisor.com/article.show.Adult-Day-Care-Programs-and-Costs.17148.html (accessed January 21, 2015).

Institute for Mindfulness Studies. "Living the Mindful Life." www.mindfulliving.org/Mindful_Living.html (accessed January 21, 2015).

Kay, Jennifer. "Anticipatory Grief." *Today's Caregiver.* www.caregiver.com/articles/general/anticipatory_grief.htm (accessed January 21, 2015).

Kenison, Katrina. *The Gift of an Ordinary Day: A Mother's Memoir.* New York: Grand Central Publishing, 2009, pp. 263–264, 159–160, 169.

Lorenzo, Karen. "Physical Fitness Tips for Caregivers." InfoLTC. http://www.infolongtermcare.org/physical-fitness-tips-caregivers/ (accessed January 21, 2015).

Lunde, Angela. "Alzheimer's Support Group Gets Lift from Humor, Sharing." Mayo Clinic. http://www.mayoclinic.org/diseases-conditions/alzheimers-disease/expert-blog/alzheimers-support-group/bgp-20055895 (accessed January 21, 2015).

Mace, Nancy L., and Peter V. Rabins, MD. *The 36-Hour Day: A Family Guide to Caring for Persons with Alzheimer's Disease, Related Dementing Illnesses, and Memory Loss in Later Life.* New York: Warner Books, 1981, pp. 35–36, 250, 257.

Marquardt, Gesine, PhD, et al. "Home Modifications for People with Dementia and Barriers to Implementation." *Dementia Today.* www.dementiatoday.com/home-modifications-for-people-with-dementia (accessed January 21, 2015).

Mayo Clinic. <1> "Loneliness: A Surprising Health Risk." *Mayo Clinic Health Letter*, July 2014, p. 6. http://newsnetwork.mayoclinic.org/discussion/mayo-clinic-health-letter-highlights-from-the-july-2014-issue/ (accessed January 21, 2015).

Mayo Clinic. <2> "Mindfulness Exercises: How to Get Started." http://www.mayoclinic.org/healthy-living/consumer-health/in-depth/mindfulness-exercises/art-20046356 (accessed January 21, 2015).

Mayo Clinic. <3> "The Path to Mindfulness and Gratitude." http://www.mayoclinic.org/diseases-conditions/cancer/expert-blog/mindfulness-and-gratitude/bgp-20087692 (accessed January 21, 2015).

Mayo Clinic. <4> "Positive Thinking: Stop Negative Self-Talk to Reduce Stress." http://www.mayoclinic.org/healthy-living/stress-management/in-depth/positive-thinking/art-20043950 (accessed January 21, 2015).

Mayo Clinic. <5> "Sleep Tips: 7 Steps to Better Sleep." http://www.mayoclinic.org/healthy-living/adult-health/in-depth/sleep/art-20048379 (accessed January 21, 2015).

Medicare. *Ask Medicare.* "How Can You Plan for the Future?" Medicare online. www.medicare.gov/files/ask-medicare-plan-for-the-future.pdf (accessed January 21, 2015).

Military OneSource. "When You Become Your Spouse's Caregiver." http://www. militaryonesource.mil/non-medical-counseling/after-deployment?content_ id=268719 (accessed January 21, 2015).

Minnesota Board on Aging. "Caregiver Resource Guide: Tips and Tools for Minnesota Caregivers." http://www.minnesotahelp.info/Public/documents/ CaregiverResourcesGuide.pdf (accessed January 21, 2015).

National Family Caregivers Association, http://www.ninds.nih.gov/ (accessed January 21, 2015).

National Institute on Aging, http://www.nia.nih.gov (accessed January 21, 2015).

National Public Radio. "Discovering the True Cost of At-Home Care." http:// nhpr.org/post/discovering-true-cost-home-caregiving (accessed January 21, 2015).

Neff, Kristin, PhD. "The Space Between Self-Esteem and Self-Compassion." https://www.youtube.com/watch?v=IvtZBUSplr4 (accessed January 21, 2015).

Online Medical Dictionary, www.online-medical-dictionary.org (accessed January 21, 2015).

Our Parents. "Comparing Costs for In-Home Care, Nursing Homes, Assisted Living and Adult Day Care." https://www.ourparents.com/articles/comparing_ costs_in_home_care_nursing_homes_and_assisted_living_and_adult_day_care (accessed January 21, 2015).

Pacific Northwest Extension Service. "Coping with Caregiving: How to Manage Stress When Caring for Older Relatives." http://ir.library.oregonstate.edu/xmlui/bitstream/handle/1957/20718/pnw315. pdf (accessed January 21, 2015).

Pekker, Michael. "10 Scoring Approaches for Alzheimer's Clock Draw Test: Alzheimer's Early Detection." *Alzheimer's Review* blog. http://alzheimers-review. blogspot.com/2011/07/10-scoring-approaches-for-alzheimers.html (accessed January 21, 2015).

Pomykal, Craig. "The Emerging Role of the Hospital Patient Advocate." Professional Patient Advocate Institute blog. http://www.patientadvocatetraining. com/blogpost/634517/116603/The-Emerging-Role-of-the-Hospital-Patient-Advocate (accessed January 21, 2015).

Randall, Kenneth E., and Irene R. McEwen. "Writing Patient-Centered Functional Goals." *PT Journal.* http://ptjournal.apta.org/content/80/12/1197. short?rss=1&ssource=mfr (accessed January 21, 2015).

Robinson, Lawrence, Jeanne Segal, PhD, and Robert Segal. "Effective Communication." *Help Guide.* http://www.helpguide.org/mental/effective_ communication_skills.htm (accessed January 21, 2015).

Sage Minder. "Caregiver Isolation." http://www.sageminder.com/Caregiving/ TakingCareofYourself/CaregiverIsolation.aspx (accessed January 21, 2015).

Sasson, Remez. "The Power of Positive Thinking." Silva Mind Control. http:// www.successconsciousness.com/index_000009.htm (accessed January 21, 2015).

Segal, Jeanne, PhD, and Gina Kemp, MA. "Eating Well as You Age." *Help Guide.* http://www.helpguide.org/articles/healthy-eating/eating-well-as-you-age.htm (accessed January 21, 2015).

Sheehy, Gail. *Passages in Caregiving: Turning Chaos into Confidence.* New York: Harper Collins, 2010, pp. 12, 298.

Spencer Scott, Paula. "Wish You Could Find a More Positive Attitude? My Dad's Last Lessons." *Caring.com.* The Self-Caring section. https://www.caring.com/ blogs/self-caring/keeping-a-positive-attitude-as-a-caregiver (accessed January 21, 2015).

Stewart, Hunter. "Pill-Tracking Device Could Monitor Whether You're Taking Your Medication." *HuffPost* website, Dec. 12, 2014.

Stone, Jim, PhD. "5 Steps to a Clear Mind." *Psychology Today.* http://www. psychologytoday.com/blog/clear-organized-and-motivated/201402/5-steps-clearer-mind (accessed January 21, 2015).

Taitel, Debra. "Letting Go Is a Process, Not an Event." *Daily Muse.* http:// dailymuse.spiritlightinsight.com/2012/04/04/letting-go-is-a-process-not-an-event/ (accessed January 21, 2015).

Tartakovsky, Margurita, MS. "Caregiving: Taking Care of Your Spouse and Yourself." *Psych Central.* http://psychcentral.com/blog/archives/2012/03/08/caregiving-taking-care-of-your-spouse-yourself/ (accessed January 21, 2015).

University of Minnesota Extension Network. "Rewards of Caregiving." http://www.extension.org/pages/9324/rewards-of-caregiving (accessed January 21, 2015).

U.S. Department of Agriculture, http://www.choosemyplate.gov/ (accessed January 21, 2015).

U.S. Department of Health and Human Services, Centers for Medicare & Medicaid Services. "Medicare Coverage of Durable Medical Equipment and Other Devices." http://www.medicare.gov/Pubs/pdf/11045.pdf (accessed January 21, 2015).

Veninga, Robert, MD. *A Gift of Hope: How We Survive Our Tragedies.* New York: Little, Brown and Company, 1985, pp. 135–148.

Volpe, Mike. "The Art of Care Receiving." *Real Living with Multiple Sclerosis.* http://www.mult-sclerosis.org/news/Apr2002/ReceivingCare.html (accessed January 21, 2015).

Warner, John, PhD. "How to Listen Attentively." *Ready to Manage.* http://blog.readytomanage.com/how-to-listen-attentively/ (accessed January 21, 2015).

Wilde, Oscar. "Quotations by Author." *The Quotations Page.* http://www.quotationspage.com/quotes?Oscar_Wilde (accessed January 22, 2015).

WebMD. <1> "Annual Physical Exams." http://www.webmd.com/a-to-z-guides/annual-physical-examinations (accessed January 21, 2015).

WebMD. <2> "Caregiving Assessment." http://www.webmd.com/healthy-aging/guide/physical-care-needs (accessed January 21, 2015).

WebMD. <3> "Caregiving and Your Loved One's Health." http://www.webmd.com/healthy-aging/guide/caregiving-tips-supporting-your-loved-ones-health (accessed January 21, 2015).

WebMD. <4> "Heart Disease: Recognizing Caregiver Burnout." http://www.webmd.com/heart-disease/guide/heart-disease-recognizing-caregiver-burnout (accessed January 21, 2015).

WebMD. <5> "Nutrition for Seniors: A Caregiving Primer." http://www.webmd.com/alzheimers/senior-nutrition (accessed January 21, 2015).

WebMD. <6> "Urinary Incontinence Products for Men." http://www.webmd.com/men/guide/urinary-incontinence-products-for-men (accessed January 21, 2015).

Wegenast, Scott. "Caregiving: Are There Boundaries?" AARP–Kentucky. http://states.aarp.org/caregiving-are-there-boundaries/ (accessed January 21, 2015).

Women's Health. "Caregiver stress fact sheet." http://www.womenshealth.gov/publications/our-publications/fact-sheet/caregiver-stress.html (accessed January 21, 2015).

About the Author

Harriet Hodgson

Author Harriet Hodgson was her mother's caregiver for nine years and became her twin grandchildrens' guardian and caregiver in 2007 when their parents were killed in separate car crashes. (Their mother was Harriet and John's elder daughter.) In 2013, Harriet became a caregiver again when her husband's aorta dissected. Her husband, John, is a retired Mayo Clinic physician. Caring for three generations—her mother, husband, and grandchildren—gave Harriet the rich experiences and wisdom that she shares with you in this book.

Hodgson has been a freelance writer for more than thirty-six years, and is the author of thirty-four published books and thousands of articles. She is a member of the Association of Health Care Journalists, Association for Death Education and Counseling, and Minnesota Coalition for Death Education and Support. In addition, she is a Contributing Writer for the Open to Hope Foundation website, The Grief Toolbox website, and The Caregiver Space website.

Hodgson has appeared on more than one hundred seventy talk shows, including CBS Radio, and dozens of television stations, including CNN. A popular speaker, she has given presentations at public health, Alzheimer's, and bereavement conferences. Hodgson speaks to community groups about caregiving, healing from grief, and creating personal happiness. Her work is cited in *Who's Who of American Women*, *World Who's Who of Women*, *Contemporary Authors*, and other directories.

About the Medical Consultant

C. John Hodgson MD, MPH

Retired Mayo Clinic physician Dr. C. John Hodgson is the medical consultant for this book. He had a long and distinguished career as a specialist in aerospace medicine, internal medicine, and public health. He did his undergraduate work at Dartmouth College, earned his MD degree from the University of Minnesota (Minneapolis), and his Master's Degree in public health from the University of California (Berkeley). He earned his specialty certification in aerospace medicine from the U.S. Air Force School of Aerospace Medicine at Brooks Air Force Base in Texas, and at the NASA Manned Spacecraft Center in Houston.

As part of his Mayo Clinic practice, Dr. Hodgson was medical director for Northwest Airlines. He was a U.S. Air Force flight surgeon for twenty-one years and is a veteran of the Vietnam War. Hodgson was head of Employee Health at Mayo Clinic's St. Mary's Hospital for a dozen years, served as president of the North Central Medical Association, secretary of the Airlines Medical Directors Association, and president of the Airlines Medical Directors Association.

Index